LOVING
in the
MOMENT

LOVING

in the

MOMENT

Moving *from*

Ego *to* Essence

in

Relationships

GINA LAKE

HAMPTON ROADS
PUBLISHING COMPANY, INC.

Cover and text design by Frame25 Productions
Cover art by Bezmaski, c/o Shutterstock.com

Hampton Roads Publishing Company, Inc.
Charlottesville, VA 22906
www.hrpub.com

Library of Congress Cataloging-in-Publication Data
is available upon request.

ISBN: 978-1-57174-627-6

Printed in the United States of America
TS

10 9 8 7 6 5 4 3 2 1
Printed on acid-free paper.

CONTENTS

ACKNOWLEDGMENTS

I'm most grateful to my husband, Nirmala, for his ongoing support and for being the model of relationship for this book and the understanding it presents. It's easy to be in relationship with someone who recognizes you as One while celebrating the differences between you.

I am also so grateful for my inner teacher, who gave me these teachings, and for life itself and the masterful way it points us toward the truth. This book is the result of a collaboration between the wisdom of this inner teacher and my knowledge, training, understanding, and experience. Much appreciation also goes to my wonderful agent, Bill Gladstone, for finding the perfect home for this book and to Robert Friedman of Hampton Roads, whose insightful suggestions made this a better book.

G. L.
January 2010

INTRODUCTION

Our ideas, both conscious and unconscious, are the main interference in love. They keep us from loving, and they create a lens through which we view the other—a lens that is often muddied by misconceptions, hurt, fear, and past relationships, including those with parents. We see the other not as he or she actually is, but as we suppose he or she is. The other, of course, does the same. Many books have been written about this phenomenon because it is at the heart of most relationship difficulties.

This book is not about analyzing and clearing away the projections, judgments, and other conditioning that interfere with relationships. To love others, we don't have to eliminate our conditioning and projections; we just have to drop into the core of our Being, where Oneness and love exist, and be with the other person from there. We just have to give our attention to love rather than to our judgments and other conditioning. It isn't difficult, but it does require a willingness on our part, and therein lies the challenge.

To do these things, we have to be willing to see that the state of mind from which we ordinarily see the world—the egoic state of consciousness—is not the best place, nor the only place, from which to live. There is another possibility, and that is to live from a deeper place—from Essence, or the divine Self that is living this life through us.

Essence has intentions for us in this lifetime, and they often involve relationships with others. If we remain in the egoic state of consciousness and attached to our conditioning, we might miss out on the relationships.

Essence intends for us. A meaningful relationship is possible, but to find it, we have to be willing to approach relationship from Essence rather than from the ego.

The ego—who we *think* we are, with all the judgments, conditioning, and projections—is an imposter, and this imposter is the saboteur of all relationships and of happiness in general. The ego is the false, or conditioned, self (as opposed to the true Self, or Essence). It is made up of conditioning—beliefs, opinions, judgments, "shoulds," and any number of ideas that are part of our programming and psychological makeup. This conditioning affects how we see and react to the world, and we often respond unconsciously to it without realizing that we have a choice. The ego is the voice in our head that admonishes and pushes us, chats with us, judges, fantasizes, and tells us what to do and how to do it. It is also behind most sentences that begin with *I*. It is the ongoing inner commentary we all are so familiar with. This aspect of the mind is often referred to as the *egoic mind,* and it is apart from the more functional mind that we use to read, learn, compute, analyze, and so forth. The ego tells us how to run our life, but it doesn't have the wisdom to guide us. Instead, it is the cause of suffering because its voice is so often negative and leads to negative feelings. Its perceptions and values are too limiting and narrow to encompass the truth about life. It's an archaic aspect of ourselves that we no longer need and are evolving beyond.

Essence, on the other hand, knows how to live this life perfectly, and it does so with love and grace. So let us explore the possibility of relating to others from Essence and how to move from the ego to Essence and find a truly meaningful relationship. While romantic relationships are the primary focus, the principles can be applied to any kind of relationship.

1

LETTING THERE BE TWO

Ego and Essence

To understand relationships, we have to start with who we really are. We can't really know another if we don't know ourselves. The difficulty in knowing the other is misunderstanding who he or she is. We take others at their word: They tell us what they do and what they like, and we think we know them. We think that's who they are. The problems begin there because, depending on what we do and what we like, we have lots of ideas about whether we like the fact that they do or don't do something, or like or don't like something.

So we need to get back to basics, back to the essential Self—*Essence,* what is behind the mask of who someone says he or she is and who we say we are. What is behind the mask is the same from one person to the next because there is only one Being here! That is the most basic truth of life: one Being is creating all of this—all of these different expressions of life. There's only one Being here, and not only are you *it,* but everyone and everything else is also it. Let this sink in a moment. What would your life be like if you really took in this truth and knew it in your bones? What if you knew that the other was your very self and, moreover, that the other was the divine Self?

This truth is very difficult to see because we are programmed to see ourselves and others as separate entities. Furthermore, we operate through a body-mind that is programmed to experience differences as a potential threat. The ego—the aspect of ourselves that appears to be running the show and using our mind to do it—is deeply conditioned, *or programmed,* to react to differences as alien to itself and therefore potentially dangerous. It views others as a threat to its survival, and yet it needs others to survive.

What a dilemma and interesting situation we find ourselves in. As long as we see ourselves as the ego and the mind, we are bound to feel tension between ourselves and others, especially when we perceive differences. Since every person is entirely unique from every other, this tension is nearly ongoing. We experience occasional relief from it when we meet someone who is similar to us in some way, or when we think someone is similar, but eventually the differences show up.

The ego feels that it must do something about these differences. It points them out, judges them, argues with them, attacks them, and tries to change them. Differences make the ego feel superior, inferior, defensive, frightened, or angry—not loving, kind, compassionate, or even curious. For the ego, differences stir up inner and outer conflict and plenty of feelings. This is the ego's experience of relationships.

For the ego, relationships are difficult and stressful, and other people are never quite right. "If only . . . ," it dreams. It's sure the problem is that the right person just hasn't come along: "If only the right person would come into my life, then I could relax and live happily ever after." Even those in relationships often secretly dream of another more perfect relationship.

This is the way the ego deals with every aspect of life, not only relationships: It longs and hopes for a better this and a better that. It's never satisfied with life, no matter what life brings. It sees life as falling short no matter what happens, and it sees relationships this way as well. As long as our identity is tied up with the ego and its servant, the egoic mind, we will never be satisfied with life or with our relationships.

Fortunately, we are not our ego or our mind. We are only programmed to think we are. Once you see this, you can begin to experience your true Self—Essence—and live your life and carry on your relationships from there. From Essence, true love is entirely possible. But it is not possible from the ego. What does the ego know about love? It knows only about protecting its interests, and there's no room for that in true love.

Love Is Recognizing the Divine Self

Love flows when we recognize our own divine Self in another. It flows when we are able to see beyond (or behind) the egoic mask to the real Self, which is exquisitely lovable and which evokes love. All the qualities we love in another are qualities of the divine Self, of Essence: compassion, understanding, wisdom, kindness, love, patience, and inner strength.

These are not qualities of the ego, which is innately self-centered and focused on its needs. Where are the wisdom, compassion, and love in that? Is it any wonder that when you are identified with the ego, you don't feel very lovable? The ego is not very lovable, but Essence is; and from Essence, even the ego is lovable.

The ego doesn't know how to love, but the divine in us—Essence—does. Essence loves. It's also wise, understanding, kind, compassionate, sensitive, patient, and caring. Anything you would want a lover or another human being to be comes from Essence, not from the ego.

The love that the ego has to offer is tainted by self-interest. "What's in it for me?" lingers in the background of every interaction between egos. This is not love, but manipulation disguised as love or kindness. It may be better than undisguised manipulation, but it's still not love in its purest sense.

Pure love can only come from our true nature—Essence, which is unadulterated goodness. Essence loves because it feels good to love and for no other reason. Why does it feel good to love? Why wouldn't you love yourself, your own creation? Just as a mother and father love their child, the divine Self loves all of creation—and especially the uniqueness of every creation. Essence loves because it is its nature to love. And we love because it is our nature to love.

The ego is the aspect of ourselves that has difficulty loving because loving makes it feel vulnerable. Loving someone gives that person power, and the ego wants to be the one with the power and control. If we love someone, that person presumably has the power to hurt and disappoint us, and the ego doesn't relinquish this power easily.

And yet the ego has a need to be loved, so it *is* vulnerable. Love stretches the ego. Without a need for love, the ego could stay comfortably separate from others. It wouldn't have to reach out to others or act any differently than it does. But because the ego needs love, it must learn to love—and that ultimately leads to its demise. The ego and love can't inhabit the same space. One must go.

From One to Two

Our nature is Oneness. We are one with everything that exists, but we have been programmed to feel separate rather than to feel our Oneness. Oneness is what we are here to discover, and oddly enough, it's discovered, in part, through twoness.

The Oneness that we are is differentiated into twoness, threeness, fourness, fiveness, and so on until it fills the universe with diversity and uniqueness. It rejoices in this diversity because this provides a means for exploring and interacting with itself in limitless ways, which were not possible as Oneness.

However, it could only have these experiences by creating a means for forgetting that Oneness, for how else could the illusion of separateness be maintained? It accomplished this illusion by programming the mind to believe that it is a separate entity. So the experience of the other is created—programmed.

It's possible, nevertheless, to wake up out of this programming and recognize our Oneness, and doing so is our destiny. We are all destined to rediscover our Oneness, but first, we must experience separation. This separation is painful because it's maintained by an egoic mind that doesn't love, so we are separate not only from the experience of Oneness, but also from the experience of love—except in those moments when we aren't.

True love, from our true nature, bleeds through into this sense of separation and beckons us back to our natural state. We eventually return to Oneness but with awareness and appreciation of our individuality and uniqueness. We bring what we have learned through the experience of separation back to the Oneness that we are. We return to Oneness wiser for having been creators in this reality. Love is what breaks the spell of the egoic state of consciousness and releases us from the prison of separation. It's love from others—from relationship—that ultimately frees us.

The Role of Relationships in Spiritual Evolution

Relationships bring us back Home to Essence because they are where we can most easily experience love. Despite the challenges they pose, relationships are also the arena in which love is developed. Perhaps that's why they are so challenging. The ego both wants love and chafes against it because love threatens its existence. The ego can't coexist with love because love is not part of its nature. When we are expressing love, we are aligned with Essence, not the ego.

Love breaks through in relationships because Essence breaks through in relationships. Essence also breaks through and is expressed in many other moments of life, but it has more opportunities to be experienced in relationship because the desire for relationship creates an openness to love. Because the ego needs relationships (and therefore love) to survive, it's open to love in the context of relationships more than in any other context.

In other circumstances, the ego attempts to maintain power, control, and superiority; however, these don't bring it what it wants in relationships. Relationships characterized by power and control provide some security, but they don't fulfill the deeper human need to love and be loved, which is a spiritual need. To return Home, we need to learn to love. We are programmed to return to Essence through love, just as we are programmed to feel separate. What an interesting paradox this is!

Relationships are also the arena in which many of our lessons are learned. Those who are most different from us provide the biggest challenges, while those who are more similar are the ones we feel most comfortable with and can more easily love. If we could always choose whom to spend time with, we would probably choose those who are most similar to us. But many of our relationships are thrust upon us and not chosen, and those relationships become the grist for our mill. Family relationships, in particular, serve this function, as do work relationships.

Many of the differences we experience between ourselves and others can be explained by soul age, which is determined by the number of lifetimes we have lived. Any relationship between two people of very different soul ages is bound to be challenging. Younger souls (those who have had fewer lifetimes) have a different way of viewing the world and different lessons than older souls. Younger and older souls live in two different worlds, in a sense, and when their worlds intersect, conflict or disappointment nearly always arises.

There's no way around the challenges caused by differences in soul age, and there isn't meant to be. We are here to experience differences and the resulting conflict because that's one way we learn to love. The pain of difficult relationships motivates us to overcome our barriers to loving. We learn to see what is lovable in others rather than what is not lovable. We fall in love with their Essence and learn to overlook their imperfections and ego.

The more lovable their personality and ego are, the easier this is to do. Some people have a more refined ego and personality. Their ego and personality have become more civilized and positive. They have learned to be kind, polite, and considerate, even though this behavior goes against the ego's nature. When people behave kindly and lovingly, Essence is expressing itself through them, and they are easy to love as a result.

Those who don't express Essence much are more difficult to love. They don't express much love, so it isn't returned to them, and they become caught in somewhat of a vicious cycle. The only way to break this vicious cycle is to become more loving. But how do you do that, especially if you don't feel loving?

Faking it helps. This may sound strange, but acting loving breaks the cycle because others often can't tell if you are actually feeling love or not. If you behave lovingly, others respond lovingly, regardless of whether or not you actually feel loving. This could be thought of as practicing good behavior, which is always a good policy in society and why it's stressed so much. Whether good behavior comes from actual goodness or not is not as important as the behavior itself. Naturally, it's even better if the behavior flows from love and goodwill. But if it doesn't, it's still preferable to bad or indifferent behavior, which reaps bad or indifferent responses from others. As a result, the ego does learn to behave well even if it doesn't feel loving, which eventually leads to behavior that flows more naturally from love. Loving is learned, mostly as a result of being loved.

We learn to love by being loved, which makes us feel safe and secure enough to open our heart to another. Anything less keeps the ego on guard and defensive. Love disarms the ego like nothing else. It breaks through the egoic state of consciousness and evokes love in us, which brings us into alignment with Essence and with the other qualities of Essence: peace, joy, serenity, happiness, kindness, compassion, patience, and fortitude, to name a few. That is why love is the greatest gift we can give another. Love is the gift that allows others to relax and return to Essence and the true happiness and peace that is our birthright. Even loving acts and words that only mimic Essence can do this. Love is so powerful that even a little bit is potent enough to change our consciousness and the consciousness of others.

The Personality Is a Costume

We naturally think of ourselves first, not others. We are trained to consider how others feel and what they need, but doing this doesn't come naturally to the ego. The ego's tendency is to start every sentence with *I*. Even when it's talking with another, it's all about *I*. Even when the conversation seems to be about the other, *I* comes in every chance it gets. Conversations between egos are dominated by *I*: *I like, I don't like, I want, I don't want, I will, I won't*.

When we relate to others, we not only relate from *I*, but we also relate to the *I* of the other. We try to find out what the ego dressed up as that particular personality is like. We want to know how he or she sees life and what he or she wants, likes, has been in the past, and dreams of being in the future. This, we think, is who that person is. We don't realize that all of these things only scratch the surface of who that person is.

We mistake the persona (including the appearance), the personality, and the ego for who someone is. These are parts of who someone is, but they are really more of a costume than anything of substance or significance. We make the persona, personality, and ego more important than they are, as if they are who someone is. This is so obvious once it's pointed out, and yet, because we are programmed to think this way, we are taken in by the exterior—the costume.

We are told to look beyond appearances, but usually that implies seeing beyond appearances to the personality. However, how people behave and react—their personality—is still part of the costume. The personality has no more depth or significance in terms of who they are than their physical appearance. We think we are being less superficial by loving people for their personality rather than their appearance, but the personality is just more programming. People have no more control over it than they do over their appearance.

The personality is not the real Self, or Essence, although the personality can be a vehicle for it. More often, the personality is a vehicle for the ego. Whether it is a vehicle for Essence or the ego, it's still just a vehicle—a means for interfacing with the world. The personality itself has nothing to do with who we really are; it's merely a useful tool in this physical reality. It helps bring about the lessons and experiences we chose before coming into this life, and it may help our soul accomplish what it set out to do. It's not who we are, and in most people, it reflects Essence only occasionally. For the most part, the personality is expressed by the ego and only occasionally by Essence. As we evolve, Essence is increasingly expressed through the personality, since that's the goal of spiritual evolution.

Every personality is unique. Think about that. What an amazing thing it is that there isn't anyone, nor will there ever be anyone, exactly like you. Your appearance, personality, talents, circumstances, life purpose, and current and past life experiences are entirely unique. No one else is designed to have the experiences you are having through your body-mind and personality. That makes your life very precious, and it makes every other life very precious too, regardless of how another may seem to us. Even the seemingly lowliest or most evil person serves evolution by having an entirely unique experience, one that will never come again. For this reason alone, all life is precious.

This uniqueness is lovable. You can learn to feel love for anyone by loving their uniqueness. That's what the Oneness finds lovable, and when you are aligned with Essence, so do you. By choosing to look beyond the qualities you don't like or respect in others to their uniqueness, you can experience love in their presence. But you have to want to experience love before you will choose to do this.

The Ego Rejects Differences

The ego doesn't want to love as much as it wants to be right, and it tries to be right by judging others. It gets pleasure in feeling superior by judging others. That pleasure is the trade-off the ego gets for love. It's not nearly as pleasurable as the joy of loving, but it's safer, and the ego generally prefers safety to love. When safety depends on love, the ego must choose love, but it prefers judgment.

Judgment is the easiest thing to do because it's the most natural thing for the ego. It's also easy because judgment is based on differences, and differences are everywhere. Life doesn't duplicate itself, so everything and everyone is an opportunity for judgment. Every difference is an opportunity for the ego to define itself as superior in some way. It pulls out a rule (conditioning) it has stored away and applies it to someone as a means of declaring that person inferior: "Doesn't she know any better than to feed her kids that junk?" "What kind of person would park like that?" "How could anyone be that stupid to pay so much for that!"

The ego takes great pleasure in such declarations because they make it feel right and, therefore, superior. Notice how much pleasure you get when you think you're right about something, especially when you are *sure* you're right. The ego doesn't actually have to be right to feel superior; it just has to *think* it's right to get this good feeling. Therefore, an enormous amount of pretending to know and pretending to be right goes on to uphold this feeling of superiority. We spin our judgments into stories to make us feel superior: "I'd never assume someone would take care of me like that prima donna does." "I know that relationship will never work—he's too fickle." "I know what it takes to get the job done, and he isn't smart enough."

We define ourselves and our values and assume others are wrong for defining themselves and their values differently. We assume that being different is wrong, bad, or at least inferior, without realizing that the standard by which we judge others is our own flawed conditioning. Rather than examining our conditioning (or just letting it be as it is), we would rather make ourselves superior because of it or try to change others to be like us. The ego doesn't allow there to be two different people, which is why the ego has trouble with relationships.

The ego doesn't celebrate differences in relationships; it seeks to annihilate or, at the very least, repudiate the differences, unless they are differences the ego admires. Some differences are okay with the ego because they are in keeping with its aspirations. For example, someone who isn't strong or rich or educated or well dressed may befriend those who are because he or she wants to become that way. However, only Essence is willing to consider differences as just what they are without putting a positive or negative value on them.

Unlike the ego, Essence sees differences as an obvious and natural part of relationships and something that enriches experience. The ego, on the other hand, feels differences between people are problematic and need to be done away with, or it simply rejects people who are different. Many never come to know those who are very different from themselves because of this tendency to discount or ignore them. People move in circles with those who are like-minded and of a similar class and rarely travel outside their circle: The wealthy hang out with the wealthy. Beer drinkers hang out with beer drinkers. Pot smokers hang out with pot smokers. Fundamentalists hang out with fundamentalists. New Agers hang out with New Agers. That way, their values are reinforced and supported, and there's less need to question who they are and how they choose to live. The ego doesn't like to have its self-image and lifestyle challenged by those who see things differently.

Essence Loves Differences

Essence enjoys differences because they make life what it is. Differences make the world go around. They create a variety of perspectives, experiences, possibilities, and opportunities. They stretch us and cause us to look more deeply—beneath the persona, the personality, and the ego—to what's living the life. If we are to get along with those who are very different from us, we have to find some commonality. In the absence of any commonality is Essence, which is what unites us all. We are united by the fact that there's no real separation, only apparent separation.

It's an illusion that we are separate at all. There's only one Being pretending to be many, all dressed up in infinite guises. This Being is immensely enjoying the costume party, and the more diverse and interesting the characters are, the better. There is obviously no room for sameness in creation because sameness just doesn't exist, not even in leaves or snowflakes. What there *is* room for is diversity. That's Essence's point of view, but it's not the ego's.

The ego's lack of appreciation for diversity puts it at odds with life. At every turn, it opposes life because it opposes diversity and differences. That's what we are here to unlearn. We are here to overcome this aversion to life as it is and to learn, instead, to embrace its unpredictability and diversity. We are not here to shape and mold it to our view, but to shape our view to it. Our *view* of life must change, not life itself. But that kind of transformation comes only through life itself, which teaches us that we can't have our way; rather, we must let life have its way with us.

Letting Life Have Its Way

Only from Oneness—from Essence—are we able to let there be two different people because Oneness likes twoness. After all, it created diversity for its enjoyment and evolution. Oneness takes joy in twoness because twoness is interesting and unpredictable (unlike Oneness), and unpredictability is fun and challenging. Why do we like games of skill? Because the outcome is unpredictable, and that's fun.

We usually don't think of unpredictability as being fun because that isn't what the ego considers fun. It likes predictability because it favors safety and security over fun. Sometimes unpredictability turns out badly, but part of the fun for Essence is turning that negative into something else—making lemonade out of lemons. From the standpoint of Essence, anything has the potential for enjoyment. Anything can produce joy for Essence. Nothing is too difficult or too horrific to be joyous. Unbelievable, you say? It makes no sense to the mind that something horrific is capable of producing joy, even in the midst of it, and yet joy exists in *every* moment. That's the truth, whether the ego accepts that or not.

Even in very wonderful moments, the egoic mind makes it difficult to experience joy because of what it says about whatever is happening. What we tell ourselves about whatever is happening has the potential to either sap the joy out of the moment or drop us into the joy that is there. Any judgment, complaint, negative evaluation, or resistance to the moment causes us to recoil from it, and that's painful and joyless.

We suffer when we divorce ourselves from the moment, because the moment—even difficult or challenging moments—is where true joy and happiness exist. Even the moment of death (either ours or someone else's), which we usually think of as the ultimate in bad moments, can be blissful if we are present to it. Fearfully anticipating death isn't pleasant, but if we are doing that, we aren't in the moment. Instead, we're in our head and agreeing with the egoic mind, which resists that moment just like every other one.

The beauty of the moment is difficult for the ego to see. It doesn't perceive beauty as much as its *ideas* about the moment, which nearly always oppose something, if not everything, about the moment. The ego is programmed to find fault with whatever is going on. It finds fault with people, and it finds fault with experiences. It's programmed this way because this provides the grist for our evolution. Saying no to whatever *is* creates the suffering that eventually causes us to choose more wisely, and learning to choose wisely is what spiritual evolution is all about.

We are programmed to choose unwisely so that we discover the wisdom of choosing otherwise. In this way, we discover love. We learn to love as a result of this programming. We don't come into life knowing how to love; we have to learn how to love. That's the setup, and the ego doesn't like this either. But no matter. Liking or not liking something is irrelevant to the unfolding of life. Have you noticed?

Life unfolds as it will regardless of whether we like what's happening or not. By opposing life, we eventually learn this truth. We learn how impotent our opposition to life is and that this opposition causes only suffering. What's left is choosing to agree with life—to love whatever is, no matter what that looks like.

That is the secret to life. It's both simple and difficult. Oneness likes a challenge, so something being difficult isn't a problem for it. It welcomes the difficult challenge of waking up out of the egoic state of consciousness. That has been Oneness's intention all along, and the suffering caused by our inability to make life turn out as we would like is how Oneness accomplishes its goal. Our desire to stop suffering eventually leads to our saying no to the ego and choosing love instead.

How Ideas and Images Interfere with Relationships

Part of letting life have its way is letting others be the way they are—letting there be two different people. Letting others be here in all their glory (or otherwise) makes it possible to have a relationship with them. However, rather than doing that, we tend to relate to our ideas about them instead of to the reality, not only the reality of what they are actually presenting to us, but also the real reality—their true Self.

Often when we relate to others, we relate to them like we related to our mother, father, ex-girlfriend or ex-boyfriend, brother, sister, teacher, boss, or anyone else they remind us of. In between yourself and others stand many others who represent your conditioning, who have shaped your way of looking at others and how you see others.

We don't see others clearly, but through a veil created by ideas that came from the people and other forces responsible for our conditioning. We have images of what we think people of a certain age, race, shape, gender, and nationality are like. We don't see people's fullness and complexity and their uniqueness. We relate to our stereotype of them. When we see an older person, we see only the oldness and relate to that person according to our ideas about being old. When we see a person of color, we see only the color of his or her skin and relate to that person according to our ideas about that race. When we see an overweight person, it stirs up our feelings and beliefs about excess weight, and we may notice nothing else about that person. We dehumanize people this way, and when taken to the extreme, this incomplete view of them can become a reason to neglect or harm them.

When we see someone, he or she evokes certain ideas, images, beliefs, and other conditioning. For example, if someone has a mustache, you might say to yourself, "Who does he think he is? He thinks he's macho." Or you assume he's macho. The truth is, who knows? You don't know who he thinks he is, why he has a mustache, or whether he is macho or not. You don't know these things, and in fact, they are irrelevant to who he really is. A mustache is part of the costume, and costumes are designed to conceal the Real and represent an image—a self-image. The self-image isn't real—it's only an image, an idea. To know someone, we have to look deeper, and when we do, we find the same blessed divinity in everyone.

Based on its beliefs and conditioning, the ego assumes it knows someone. For instance, the ego might assume an overweight person is lazy or undisciplined, despite the many examples to the contrary. The ego assumes it knows because it's uncomfortable with not knowing, so it makes something up. It pretends to know. To the ego, its assumptions are as good as really knowing, as long as it can convince itself that it knows. The ego isn't interested in truth, only in feeling safe and in being right, and pretending to know is good enough for this because the ego is very willing to be convinced by its own ideas and beliefs. Most of the time, it doesn't even have to be convinced. Most people are so unconscious of their ideas and beliefs that they don't question them, although they may fight to convince others that their ideas and beliefs are true. The ego is in the business of defending its ideas and convincing others, not in the business of examining its ideas.

The ego takes its ideas as the truth about someone. If the ideas prove to be untrue, it quickly forgets its mistake and forms new assumptions. The ego doesn't dwell on its mistaken ideas, but instantly comes up with others. It never actually examines its ideas; it just replaces the old ones with new ones and continues to believe in something. For the ego to believe nothing—to not know—is much more uncomfortable than getting something wrong, because it's very forgiving of its own mistakes. Besides, most of the time, it *believes* it's right, and that's good enough for it.

There isn't anything wrong with ideas intervening between us and reality. Life is programmed to be this way. It's just that this programming interferes with our ability to have good relationships and, therefore, to love, so eventually we must realize the effects of this programming.

We will continue to see others through the lens of the ego's assumptions as long as we are identified with the ego. As long as we think of ourselves as the one who is having these thoughts, we will be convinced that these thoughts are true, and we will be deeply involved in the self-deception and delusion of the ego. The only way out is to recognize that you *have* an ego, but you are not the ego. How simple that sounds! It's profoundly simple to see this, really. It's just not simple to live as if you are not the ego because we are programmed to think of ourselves as this *I* that has all these ideas, beliefs, and opinions. And yet every idea, belief, and opinion—nearly every thought—is part of our programming.

The Self-Image Is Manufactured

Most of the programming that goes on in the mind is designed to create a self-image and images about others as well. The egoic mind creates images—ideas—about everything, but it is particularly designed to create a self-image, because what else is the ego if not an image? The ego creates itself by describing itself a certain way: *I am this, I like this, I want this, I think this, I did this.*

Our self-image is entirely manufactured. It's created by our programming and influenced by our conditioning. It's always changing because our conditioning is always changing. That doesn't make it more real, only less real. What is Real (Essence) doesn't change. What is Real is here in this moment *and* in the next. It's what doesn't come and go, as the Indian sage Ramana Maharshi so simply put it. Who we really are is what doesn't come and go.

As long as you believe you are your self-image and that others are their self-image or your image of them, you will find it difficult to have relationships. From the level of ego, relationships boil down to a struggle to change others and get our needs met. For the ego, relationships, like everything else, are all about *me* and what's in it for *me*. What happens when this is the basis for a relationship? No one is happy. No one gets what he or she wants because getting what the ego wants misses the point.

Relationships are not about getting what we want, but about giving to another for the joy of giving. But what does the ego know about giving to another simply for joy? That's Essence's domain. Relationships are an opportunity to learn the joys of giving, but that happens infrequently when we are in the grips of ego identification. Fortunately, relationships have a way of opening our hearts and allowing Essence to be expressed, and Essence expresses itself through kindness, caring, love, and giving.

Once the joy of loving and giving is experienced, the desire for more love and joy is ignited, and we learn to overcome the ego's selfishness and self-centeredness. Relationships help us wake up out of identification with the ego because they show us the joy of loving and giving—the joy of Essence—and we begin to want that joy more than we want our conditioned ideas and needs met.

Then it's possible to have a real relationship with someone—a relationship between what is Real in someone and Real in another. This is the ideal in relationship—not finding an ideal partner who will meet our every need, but *being* the ideal partner by being the expression of loving kindness that we have always wanted and that we have always been. We become that ideal, loving partner by being aligned with Essence.

Programming and Relationships

It's not that you ever get to a point where the personality, the physical appearance, and the ego don't play a part in relationships, because they always will. We are programmed to be attracted to certain physical features and personalities. This programming is wide ranging, so there are many possibilities for relationship for everyone.

We are also programmed to have certain experiences through relationships, so we find ourselves responding in certain ways in relationships. You might be fearful or fearless, distrusting or trusting, giving or withholding, sexy or not sexy, affectionate or not affectionate, controlling or allowing, independent or dependent. These different ways of being result in our having certain experiences and learning certain things, which is the reason for the programming.

We are also programmed to have certain types of relationships because each type is an opportunity to learn something different. For instance, some are programmed to have a variety of shorter relationships rather than a single, long-term one. Some are programmed to not have many relationships and instead channel energy into careers, creativity, or something else. Some are programmed for monogamous relationships, and some aren't. Some are programmed for heterosexual relationships, and some aren't. For some, relationships don't have much to do with what they came into life to learn, while for others, relationships are central.

You can uncover your programming by noticing your tendencies and patterns in relationship. By paying attention to the kind of people you are attracted to, how you tend to act in relationship, and the kinds of relationships you form (e.g., savior-victim, mother-child, enmeshed, abusive, detached, platonic, unrequited, erotic, romanticized), you can come to understand your programming and any issues and lessons that may be part of that. Your programming is there to involve you in certain experiences and catalyze your growth.

Conditioning is part of this programming. Nearly everyone has psychological issues around relationships they are meant to overcome or heal, and often overcoming and healing these relationship issues can only be accomplished through relationship. In relationships we learn to trust, share, cooperate, compromise, negotiate, commit, give, love, accept, let go, serve, be loyal, be unselfish, be responsible, be intimate, and be understanding. These are just some of the many issues you may have come into this life to work on through relationships.

Life brings us the types of people and relationships we need to evolve, or heal, certain psychological issues. We do learn and evolve as a result of our relationships. We do overcome our conditioning and become more capable of having a good relationship. Overcoming conditioning, or at least becoming aware of it, is central to having a good relationship because our conditioning keeps us identified with the ego, and relationships will always be a challenge from that level. Once we stop being run by our conditioning, Essence shines through more in our relationships, and much more happiness, harmony, and joy are possible.

Essence in Relationships

Relating from Essence is very different from relating from the ego. When we relate from Essence, the dominant feeling is acceptance: You allow others to be the way they are. In fact, you celebrate how they are. This doesn't mean you might not dislike something about them, but the general feeling toward them is that everything is just right as it is. This feeling of acceptance and allowing toward another is love in its simplest and most unadulterated (by conditioning) form. In its most basic form, love is allowing: you allow the person to be exactly the way he or she is without any reservations or desires for anything to be different than it is.

Commonly in relationships, the experience of allowing lasts only a moment because the ego's job is to spoil love with *buts:* But what about the fact that he or she does this or doesn't do this? Or the fact that he or she looks this way or doesn't look that way? The ego lies in wait for the opportunity to list someone's supposed faults (according to the ego's conditioning). So it's never long before the judgments and reservations begin to flow.

However, as long as you remain in Essence, these judgments are seen as meaningless and silly. The love you feel while aligned with Essence is stronger than these *buts*—until it fades. And then the *buts* become stronger than the experience of love, and you slide into identification with the ego once again. This is a description of most moments in relationship: one moment we are aligned with Essence and feeling love; the next moment we believe the ego has a point, and we become aligned with it.

The ego's reasoning can be very seductive, and sometimes we are powerless to ignore it, usually because of our unconscious beliefs and ideas. Once we become conscious of these, it's easier to hold our own against the ego, but these beliefs and ideas must first come to the surface and be seen. This is the work that must be done, which enables us to stay in Essence for longer periods of time. Eventually we live life from Essence rather than from the ego, and we express love and acceptance most of the time.

2

MOVING BEYOND JUDGMENT

Projection

Judgment is probably the most destructive force in relationships. It maintains ego identification, which is incompatible with love and relationship. Judgment is the primary way the ego maintains its sense of being separate and superior. It puffs itself up through comparisons and judgments of others. It makes itself better than others by hauling out a rule or a conditioned belief that proves its superiority. Relationships can't thrive in such an environment. Judgment and criticism prevent love from flowering and kill it if it's already there.

When we first fall in love with someone, judgments are suspended. Not only do we see beyond any imperfections, but we also envision an even more perfect mate than is possible. In the beginning of a relationship, self-delusion abounds. And that is how the beginning of a relationship is meant to be, or how would relationships ever get off the ground? If the judgments that are present later were present in the beginning, the relationship wouldn't stand a chance.

Something happens early in romantic relationships that makes relationship possible. That something draws people into relationship, only to have them face the other's limitations and the judgments that go along with those limitations. An amazing process kicks in when we first meet someone we are attracted to, and this process allows us to see past the imperfections and see only what we want to see. This process is called projection, and it's unconscious, meaning we aren't aware of it when it is happening. In this way, projection is similar to programming, which we also are often not aware of.

Projection is a well-documented and common phenomenon, but it still isn't easy to recognize when it's happening. We have many romantic ideas and ideals that we long to have fulfilled through another, and we project these onto someone and assume he or she has these qualities. That person is usually somewhat of a match for these ideas and ideals, but sometimes only slightly or in only a few ways.

No one could possibly match every idea we have for our ideal partner because many of our ideas are unrealistic and contradictory. Even if someone has the qualities we're looking for, we still have no control over how or when they are expressed. For instance, you may love it that your partner is adventuresome, but you don't want that quality showing up when the taxes need to be done. Or you may love it that your partner loves to cook, until you realize that cooking and eating is all you ever do together. It's not enough for someone to have all the right qualities if he or she doesn't express them as we would like. It's also not enough for someone to have all the right qualities if he or she doesn't feel the same way about us! Finding a partner with all the right qualities, which are primarily features of the personality, just isn't enough to make a relationship work.

Compatibility Between Personalities

Some compatibility is important on a personality level. Because we tend to judge those whose personalities we don't like or don't get along with, similarities are important in reducing judgments. The fewer judgments we have about someone, the better our chances are for getting along. Still, all we are talking about here is compatibility between personalities, which are the programmed costumes. For a relationship to work, there has to be more than compatibility between personalities.

Our personality and what we desire in a partner are part of our programming. We can't get around this, but it isn't the whole picture; nor does compatibility on this level make for real happiness or a meaningful relationship. Two people can have very compatible personalities, but not want to be together. Out of the billions of people in the world, there are probably many we are compatible with in terms of our personalities and other conditioning, and yet finding a meaningful relationship is still quite a challenge for most. That's because there's more to a meaningful relationship than compatible personalities or meeting each other's desires.

The ego has its list of qualities and attributes it wants in a partner and in a relationship. To the ego, these seem to be reasonable and useful criteria for relationship. It can't imagine being in love with someone who doesn't fulfill most of its criteria. The ego is so sure of what it needs in relationship, and it probably does need these things to be comfortable and as happy as it can be in relationship. Nevertheless, meeting the ego's criteria isn't enough to bring real happiness because its criteria are too narrow and shortsighted. The ego lacks the vision to understand what is necessary for real happiness. It knows only what it wants, according to its conditioning, and those desires are its basis for relationship.

Relationships That Support Essence's Goals

Each of us is so much more than the ego. The ego is the false self, the conditioned self. The ego is part of our experience as human beings, and it serves our material well-being to some extent by providing us with primitive instincts for survival. But it falls short in being able to guide us as spiritual beings. We are essentially spiritual beings who have an ego and not an ego with spiritual tendencies. Consequently, happiness in relationships depends on meeting spiritual needs, which have little to do with the ego, its conditioning, and its costume, the personality. The happiest relationships are not only those in which we relate from Essence, but also those that fulfill the goals of Essence for this life.

Essence has a purpose for living this life. It is unfolding its plan through each of us. It has goals for each life, and fulfilling them brings meaning. A particular relationship either supports these goals or it doesn't. If a relationship is compatible on the personality level, but not supportive of these goals, it won't be fulfilling and it probably won't last, no matter how attractive and wonderful two people find each other to be.

Conversely, the love of your life (the love that brings the most meaning to your life) might be someone you aren't as compatible with or as attracted to as some others, but the meaningfulness of that relationship will overshadow those differences. This sense of meaning and the love it engenders can sustain two people through many difficulties and differences.

Fortunately, those we are destined to be with usually also are designed to be attractive to us and at least somewhat compatible. Nevertheless, sometimes a relationship is intended to be difficult to catalyze our growth. Because it provides the growth we long for spiritually, such a relationship can feel very fulfilling and meaningful despite the challenge it poses. So from the perspective of Essence, compatibility isn't always the goal. Incompatibility can be a useful tool for our evolution.

Judgments can prevent us from being happy in relationships that are compatible on an egoic and personality level, but, more important, they can prevent us from forming potentially meaningful relationships, ones that are destined to either help us unfold our potentials and talents or learn the lessons we came here to learn. Judgments can especially interfere with these types of relationships when compatibility and attraction are not at their highest. For superficial reasons, we may overlook a relationship that might be very fulfilling and important to our life's goals.

How Judgments Interfere with Finding a Relationship

When we are identified with the ego, being around others brings out judgments. Because the ego feels separate from others, it needs to feel superior to feel safe, so it sizes up the competition and brings the competition down to size by judging. Bringing the competition down to size allows the ego to relax a little in the company of others, but at a great cost, because there's no joy in maintaining this position. Making others small makes us feel very small and only increases our need to feel better than others. This strategy actually backfires and leaves us all the more entrenched in the egoic state of consciousness, which is a state of contraction—of feeling small and impotent. So the more we judge, the more we feel the need to judge. But judging never gets us the peace or love we long for. Here is an exercise to help you become more aware of your judgments.

EXERCISE: NOTICING JUDGMENTS

The next time you are around someone, notice how the presence of another stirs up comparisons, judgments, evaluations, and criticism. The ego sizes up others according to criteria based on conditioning. Appearance (how others look, how they are dressed, how they speak, and how they carry themselves) is usually the first thing we evaluate and judge. Next, we evaluate and judge what others say, and then we evaluate and judge how they respond or react to us.

Watch how the mind pays attention to these things nearly always in this order. It forms an initial impression based on appearance, and then it evaluates how the other person's beliefs and values (conditioning) compare to its own. On this basis, we decide whether we like someone or not. We use our conditioning to evaluate others. Those who match our conditioning are seen as kindred spirits, and those who don't are judged negatively. This is how the ego handles others. It categorizes them in relationship to itself and judges accordingly.

Given this automatic tendency to evaluate and form judgments about others before we even know them, we miss many opportunities for relationship that might be rich in many ways. Some of our most valuable relationships are with those who are different from us because they often bring in new perspectives and information, and challenge us in needed ways. Differences are stimulating and catalytic. We may not initially like those who seem different from us, and we may not like what they stir up in us, but that's no measure of their value to us or of how we might feel about them once we have come to know them.

Those who are similar to us don't challenge us, and that isn't always good for us. We can become complacent or set in our ways and even more entrenched in our conditioning and views. Those who are different from us cause us to question our beliefs and ways of looking at things, which may be very beneficial. But because we don't like our beliefs and perceptions challenged, we usually avoid these people if we can. The question is, do you want to feel comfortable more than you want to grow? You get to choose, but you can't necessarily have both comfort and growth.

Because our initial judgments narrow down the field, we end up looking for love among only those who are like us or who fulfill the requirements of our conditioning. We expect our true love to line up with our conditioning, but maybe our conditioning—what we like and dislike—isn't a good guide for finding true love. What if, instead, our conditioning *interferes* with finding true love?

It may be that you have conditioning that prevents you from finding a satisfying relationship. You may be so busy going after what you like and don't like that you don't consider that your likes and dislikes could actually be keeping you from love. Trying to find love this way is like trying to row a boat with a fishing pole: you expect something to do a job that it isn't capable of. When that happens, you have to change the tool. You may have to change the criteria you are using to search for a mate. You may need to change your conditioning—and that's no small matter.

The most effective way to change conditioning is to be around those who have different conditioning, but that won't happen if you adhere to your initial criteria for choosing a mate. Given this, it's easy to see why many don't find a relationship that is meaningful, or when they do, they don't recognize it. Most of us have programming that prevents us from having a meaningful and good relationship, and until this programming is seen and other choices are made, such a relationship may remain out of reach.

The programming that most obviously interferes with relationship is programming that limits the people we are open to being in a relationship with. This is usually accomplished by having a list of qualities and features we want in a partner and not veering from that. While it's useful to know what you like and don't like, and what you are willing to live with and not, using this list as a criterion for sorting out who you are willing to meet and get to know isn't helpful.

Although suspending initial judgments is very difficult, because they kick in automatically and immediately upon meeting someone, doing so opens up otherwise overlooked possibilities for relationship that, at the very least, might help overcome the conditioning that stands in the way of a happy relationship. In other words, you may have to kiss a lot of frogs to find your prince or princess because those frogs are blessings in disguise. Challenging relationships or ones with people who are very different from us are often just what we need to develop and prepare us for a meaningful relationship.

In this culture, conditioning is very strong around sexual attractiveness and beauty. For most, physical attractiveness is very high on our list of what we want in a partner. Attractiveness is currency in this culture; and to the ego, currency means safety, security, and survival, which it prizes above all else. So it's not surprising that qualities that provide safety and security are high on everyone's list.

EXERCISE: ASSESSING THE EGO'S CRITERIA

Make a list of all the things that seem important to you in a partner. Go over this list carefully and see if you can determine which items are requirements of your ego and which ones might be requirements of Essence. What is the difference? How can you tell the difference between a requirement of the ego and a requirement of Essence?

There is a distinctly different feel to each type of requirement. The ego is into power, success, safety, security, money, beauty, and pleasure, and it looks for a partner who can provide these. The ego isn't as concerned with specific talents or interests as with what someone else can do to improve life in terms of the values just mentioned. Essence, on the other hand, wants love, fulfillment, meaning, and connection in relationship, and it looks for a partner who can provide these. Essence also looks for a partner with talents and interests we value and a partner who values our talents and interests.

Criteria for a Relationship: The Ego's vs. Essence's

It's good to be clear about the ego's priorities because they may not be the same as Essence's. Essence often has other criteria, ones that *will* bring us happiness in relationship. The ego's list promises happiness, but doesn't deliver it. Although what the ego and Essence desire in a partner aren't always at odds, when they are, putting the ego's desires before Essence's will only delay our happiness in relationships.

The good news is that following the ego's criteria is likely to bring us the lessons we need to get beyond some of our conditioning. Through disappointment and disillusionment in relationships, we learn that the ego's criteria are not very trustworthy, and we begin to listen more to Essence and to those who speak for Essence in our lives. Here's an exercise that will help you become more aware of the criteria you hold for relationship and whether they serve the ego or Essence.

How Judgments Interfere with Sustaining Relationships

Judgments not only narrow the field of opportunities for relationship, but they sabotage relationships once you are in them. Relationships that start out rosy often end up far from that, and you are left wondering what happened. What you once loved about another is now unappealing or overshadowed by what you don't like. Now all you can see is what you don't like, not what you do.

This happens for a number of reasons. When the illusions that are part of falling in love drop away, you are left with the real person. The "warts" that were not immediately apparent are now visible. At first you saw only what you wanted to see, and now you see the truth: the beloved has qualities you don't like; the beloved is different than you.

The discovery that the beloved has qualities that you don't like is actually not the tragedy you might assume. What's so terrible about someone having qualities you don't like? We give our preferences more meaning and importance than they deserve. To the ego, someone having qualities we don't like is a call to arms, or at least a call for change. The ego is very upset by others not conforming to its desires, but this upset is really unnecessary. The ego's preferences become a problem because it wants others to conform to its preferences (conditioning), as if these likes and dislikes were the standard by which everyone should live.

The discovery of differences is a blow to the ego, and the ego deals with this blow through judgment. It judges the other person to try to get its way and make that person conform. Judgments are the ego's weapon of choice in relationships. They are the primary way the ego attempts to get its way. It attacks and tries to manipulate others by belittling them or their behavior. The criticism seems justified because it's worded in a way that makes the one who is criticizing seem superior.

For example, you realize after you move in with your beloved that he leaves things out rather than putting them away when he's done with them. But you were trained to be very neat and put things away immediately. You take pride in doing so. It's just the right thing to do, you say to yourself. So you might say to him, "I can never find what I'm looking for because you don't put stuff away. That's just rude and inconsiderate, and I'm tired of putting your things away. You try to get away with doing as little as possible around here. I'm always the one taking care of things." This judgment is designed to make him want to please you and win your love back by doing things your way. But it doesn't really have that effect, does it? In fact, it's more likely to have the opposite effect.

The ego thinks it can win through intimidation and by assuming the moral high ground (according to its conditioning). What it doesn't notice is how ineffective its judgments are in accomplishing what it wants. Rather than noticing that judging is a poor strategy for getting others to conform to what it wants, it blames the other person for not conforming to its standards and becomes all the more persistent in its criticism. Its solution to the failure of its strategy is to criticize all the more. The failure of this strategy and the unrelenting criticism creates anger and resentment in both people, each of whom is convinced that the other person is being unreasonable. From the standpoint of each person's conditioning, the other person does seem unreasonable. It feels like there's no solution, no common ground. The two of you are deadlocked, and no one is willing to budge.

Who is this *you* that is unwilling to budge? It is the conditioned you, the one who has requirements for others and for relationship based on your programming. There is another you that is much more flexible and values love above an idea or the belief that things should be a certain way. That *you* is Essence living through you.

The real you—Essence—is willing to allow the beloved to live life as he or she sees fit. It may ask for what it prefers to have happen ("Would you mind putting these things away, or do you mind if I put them away now?"), but it accepts responsibility for having this preference and doesn't belittle the beloved in an attempt to get him or her to comply. It doesn't use judgment and anger as a weapon to manipulate others.

Most disagreements are about conditioning: you think something should be a certain way and the other person disagrees. Sometimes the disagreement is over something minor, like how to make the bed, and sometimes it's over something more important, like how to handle money. Regardless of the specific issue, it's still conditioning, and as long as you attempt to solve issues by deciding whose conditioning is better, there will be problems.

In a sense, no one's conditioning is better than anyone else's, since it's still conditioning. Although some might argue that their conditioning is more sensible or efficient or healthy or whatever, others might argue the value of being sensible, efficient, healthy, or whatever. These issues can only be resolved lovingly by dropping into Essence and finding the solution from there.

The inability to resolve differences causes many relationships to crumble, either slowly or quickly. Judgment undermines relationship little by little (or more quickly), but the result is the same—the demise of the relationship. A little bit of ongoing judgment is just as bad as a lot of it, because, over time, it's enough to kill a relationship. Judgment is more pernicious than we would like to think. It seems rather innocuous in minor doses or over small matters, but like poison, a little is enough to kill when administered repeatedly over time.

Judgments That Pretend to Be Helpful

Judging isn't always an attempt to get our way. Many are aware of the tendency to use judgment in that way and don't indulge in it as they used to, but they are still not above judging for other reasons. Judgment often continues because we still think it has some value. We genuinely believe we have a duty to improve our partner by pointing out flaws, or what we consider to be flaws, according to our conditioning. We are convinced that judging someone under these circumstances is not only justifiable, but also the right thing to do.

For example, if you notice your partner isn't changing the oil in the car often enough, you might use this as an opportunity to point out this flaw ("You never remember to change the oil") or you can remind him in a way that doesn't comment on his character ("Is it time for the oil to be changed?" or "Are you planning on changing the oil soon?" or "I think it's time for the oil to be changed"). One way assumes his behavior reflects something flawed about him, and the other is simply informative and potentially helpful. These two approaches have a very different effect: one leaves him feeling bad about himself and you, which won't make him want to be helpful; the other approach leaves him feeling respected. By giving information rather than judging, you are being a good partner in taking care of life's details, which is likely to result in cooperation.

Or, for example, if you are concerned that your partner isn't eating healthfully, you might ask, "Are you having another bowl of ice cream?" This, like many questions, is a disguised judgment, which implies that your partner is eating too much ice cream. The implication isn't likely to go unnoticed. In asking questions like these, you put yourself in the position of policing your partner. That won't be appreciated, won't likely change the situation, and is only likely to inspire your partner to search his or her memory for instances when you transgressed similarly. Nothing is accomplished by such questions, no matter how well meaning you *think* they are, except an increase of tension in the relationship and contraction in each person.

Another subtle form of judgment is suggesting your partner do something to improve in ways you want him or her to improve: "Why don't you go to AA?" "Why don't you try . . . ?" "Why don't you find out about . . . ?" "Why don't you just go on a diet?" "Why don't you see a counselor about that?" "Why don't you just stop doing that?" These questions feign concern and pretend to be helpful, but they imply the partner should do these things. They assume he or she wants help in some area, but isn't able to come up with a solution—an assumption that is demeaning. They also imply you have the solution, placing you in a position of superiority, which your ego likes, but your partner's ego doesn't. Questions like these are bound to create only more resistance to any perceived problem and further tension in the relationship.

In fact, most questions that begin with "why" aren't really questions at all, but disguised judgments, complaints, or requests. For instance, when you ask, "Why did you leave your clothes on the bed?" you aren't actually wondering why the clothes are on the bed, but more subtly expressing your disapproval of them being there. You are pointing out to your partner that he or she isn't living up to your standards. You may be feeling a sense of self-righteousness around this issue, which is driving you to say something about it. The ego loves to find fault with others. Most questions that start with "why" are best left unsaid. If you want your partner to put the clothes away, then just ask nicely: "Would you mind putting your clothes away?" It helps if you can offer a legitimate reason for requesting this: "Would you mind putting your clothes away so that I can take a nap?" If you don't have a legitimate reason, maybe you could just let the clothes be there. Is having the clothes put away more important than love?

When we judge someone, we often sincerely feel we are being helpful, but this helpfulness is still the ego, just in a little friendlier guise. As we become more evolved, our ego has to become more skillful at convincing us to be on its side. It does so by appealing to our altruistic side instead of our selfish side. You can tell when the ego is using this tactic because of the self-righteousness involved. Self-righteousness is the ego's spiritual version of being right. Self-righteousness is moral rightness rather than intellectual rightness, but the intent is the same: to be superior.

We feel justified in judging our partner if it's in the name—or guise—of helping him or her be a better person. The idea that we should help our partner grow is the ego using the fact that we do grow and taking on our partner's growth as its mission. While Essence brings about this growth in its own way, according to a certain timing and plan, the ego attempts to make this growth happen on its own timetable and according to its ideas. This is just more manipulation. Who is it that wants the partner to be a better person? The ego does, of course, because our partner is a reflection of us, and we want to look good. Pushing our partner to grow is just the ego wanting its way, but disguising its judgments as spiritual guidance.

The ego is tricky. It can be difficult to see it operating in your life. Just when you think you are on top of it, it comes up with even more subtle ways to draw you into identification with it and out of identification with Essence. In many respects, the ego is engaged in a battle for your soul, but Essence isn't fighting. It's allowing the ego to do what the ego does and waiting for you to choose it over the ego. It's quietly waiting until you are tired of the suffering caused by the ego and you finally turn and give your attention to it.

The ego's position is that it's your job to change and improve your partner. Let's be clear that this isn't your job. Etch this in stone somewhere, put it on your mantel, or pin it to your refrigerator. Let it sink into the depths of your being, because it is that important. It's the ego, not Essence, that is motivated to change and improve your partner.

Life, through Essence, will change someone when and how he or she needs to be changed, and unless we are acting as a mouthpiece for Essence, we have no business trying to change someone. Any attempt to change someone else through judgment can be assumed to be our ego, because when Essence does express itself through us, it does so spontaneously and with love and acceptance—not judgment. What a relief! Not only is it not our job to change or improve our partner, but it's also not our job (or our business) to change or improve anyone else either. "Let go and let God," as they say.

Whenever you find yourself struggling with someone or with life, you are identified with the ego. Being aligned with Essence, on the other hand, is an experience of letting go—allowing. You allow things, your partner, and other people to be the way they are. What a relief it is to not have to change what is! You can just relax and enjoy it as it is. There's no problem except what the ego defines as a problem. Don't listen to it; just stay in the moment, in peace and contentment with what is. No problem, no struggle, and no effort required. Life can be easier than you think.

It's thinking that gets us into trouble. Thinking is the ego's domain, for the most part. It thinks up fantasies and scary stories to get us to get what it wants. It wastes our time and energy if we let it. Essence has other plans, and if we let go of the ego's ideas and allow Essence to express itself in our lives and relationships, everything goes so much better. Then it's possible to discover what love is really about.

Finding a Meaningful Relationship

Many people don't find a meaningful relationship because they are using the ego's criteria and overlooking possibilities that could be meaningful. The love, or loves, of your life might not match your ego's criteria very closely. This is not as big a problem as it sounds, however, because Essence has ways of overcoming the ego's rigid ideas about relationship.

These ideas, however, can still cause problems on and off once you are in a relationship with your true love. It's a rare individual who is completely done with the ego and the possibility of ego identification. Even those who live much of their lives aligned with Essence find themselves contracted and identified with the ego and its judgments at times. Some conditioning is very compelling and difficult to ignore, and it comes up in the best of relationships and must be dealt with.

The ego's list of criteria for relationship is self-defeating. Because it doesn't lead to happiness or a lasting relationship, it creates an opportunity for Essence to woo us back to itself. This unhappiness causes us to reevaluate our criteria and opens us up to Essence and other possibilities for relationship, especially ones Essence places in front of us.

If it's time for you to have a meaningful relationship, Essence makes this happen by drawing the intended person to you in some way. Essence is also able to motivate your friends or others to introduce that person to you and to speak enthusiastically about him or her. The ego is very influenced by other people's opinions, so even if someone doesn't measure up to your ego's criteria, the fact that he or she measures up to a friend's criteria might be enough to interest you in a meeting.

Today, dating services are bringing people together who might not ordinarily be open to meeting each other, and in that way, these services may be serving Essence. However, most dating services and those who use them tend to focus on the types of criteria the ego focuses on, so a lot of dating happens, but not necessarily much with real meaning.

Nevertheless, exposure to so many different people is a good way to learn about ourselves and others, which improves our chances of eventually finding love. Through dating and relationships, we hone our search criteria, and some criteria from Essence are bound to get on the list. The more our criteria are aligned with Essence, the better our chances are for finding real love.

Eventually, Essence will probably succeed at bringing you someone you can be truly happy with. But when this happens, will you recognize your good fortune? What will it feel like? Essence has ways of helping you recognize true love when it shows up, but you have to be willing to pay attention to the signs and not to your judgments. Some people miss opportunities for true love because they are too attached to and identified with their judgments to let them go. Their judgments are more important to them than love. This especially happens to those who are strongly identified with the ego and who don't trust Essence when they do experience it.

If there is a strong enough match between what you are conditioned to find attractive and the person Essence has brought you, you will probably feel the usual feelings of falling in love. These feelings aren't always present when we first meet our true love, but they usually develop at some point. Sometimes the feeling of meeting our true love is described as "love at first sight," but attraction can also cause this same feeling.

Other more intangible feelings, in addition to attraction, are likely to be present when you meet the person Essence intends for you. They are often described as feeling drawn to someone, feeling at home, feeling good with someone, feeling like you can just be yourself, and feeling like you've known someone for a long time or in another lifetime. These feelings are generally so compelling that they overshadow most judgments that might initially stand in the way of a relationship. However, once the relationship is cemented, the differences start showing up, followed by the judgments. The first time this happens, one person or the other might run because of a sense of having been deluded. If the relationship is meant to be, however, these negative feelings and judgments will be short lived and eclipsed by deep love.

When two people are meant to be together—to enjoy love and life together, to help each other, or to learn something—love is just there. Where it comes from and why is one of the great mysteries of life. You don't and can't make love happen; it just happens. It shows up, and you had nothing to do with it. Essence expresses itself in life this way. It reaches into the world of the ego, tears you away from it, and brings you Home.

Love isn't something we can understand because it's not able to be grasped by the mind. Love is not in the mind's or the ego's domain. It's a quality of Essence—of who we really are—and that is too mysterious for the mind to be able to contemplate. And the mind doesn't want to. Yet love is where fulfillment lies and why relationships are so important to us.

Your Judgments Are About You

Your judgments are not about others; they are about you and your conditioning. For example, if you are judgmental toward someone who is overweight (or toward yourself about this), that's because you have conditioning that says it's not okay to be overweight. The problem is that this judgment simply isn't true. It's okay to be overweight, especially when that's the case. It's okay simply because that's the way it is. Why argue with reality? Some people are overweight, and that's the truth. End of story. Of course, the ego is always arguing with reality, and that's why we suffer.

If seeing someone who is overweight triggers a judgment and causes you to contract, then you have an opportunity to explore any negative beliefs you have around being overweight. What meaning do you give to being overweight? What does it mean if you or someone else is overweight? Does it mean to you that he or she (or you) is a bad person? Weak? Lazy? Ignorant? Poor? Troubled? Unhappy? Unsuccessful? Uncover all the meanings you give to being overweight. Whether the ideas you have about being overweight apply to you or someone else, they cause you to contract when you believe them, and if you express them, they cause others to suffer too. Unless you want to suffer and be a source of suffering in this world, it's wise to examine any conditioning that causes you to contract. Once you discover how untrue and how unhelpful such beliefs are, they begin to lose their power to cause you and others suffering.

Just because others have the same conditioning—the same false beliefs—doesn't make that conditioning true. No one's conditioning is true, not ultimately, and no one has "the right" conditioning or beliefs. We all have our own conditioning, and no one has exactly the same conditioning, which helps explain why getting along with others is so challenging. To make things worse, we think our conditioning is true and correct, or at least better than someone else's; if we didn't, we wouldn't judge others and try to change them. We believe our conditioning is right and superior because we are programmed to believe it is right and superior.

Like a fish in water, we don't see or examine certain programmed assumptions we have as human beings. One of the deepest and most unconscious assumptions we have is that what we think is true. We live by the unquestioned assumption that if we think it, it must be true. We don't question our beliefs because they are what we think. Since everyone has different ideas (conditioning), this conviction that our beliefs are unquestionably true causes a lot of problems in relationships. A great deal of energy is expended trying to convince others of what we believe or trying to defend our ideas, when it could be much better spent.

Ideas are just ideas. They're not that important, but we are programmed to think they are because ideas create our identity—they create the *you* that you think you are. Without your ideas, beliefs, opinions, dreams, and memories, who would you be? Who is this *you* that you think you are if not a composite of ideas about who you are—your conditioning? You can test this premise that who you really are is not who you think you are in moments when thinking isn't happening: where is this *you* that you think you are, with all of its stories, history, and beliefs? For a moment this *you* stops existing, but do you still exist?

Something still exists even when you stop identifying yourself as this *you*, with all its ideas and history. This something that exists beyond thought is the real you—Essence. It's present when you are thinking too, but you don't notice it because you are lost in thought (how true that expression is!). And what are ideas? Without your belief in them, they are nothing. In and of themselves they have no power, and the truth they contain is only relative truth, not ultimate truth.

Your judgments relate to beliefs you personally hold as true. They are true to you, but not ultimately true. The beliefs you hold as true are often very different from the ones others hold as true, and no one's are ultimately true, although every ego believes its beliefs are. The best thing that can be said about any belief is that it may have more truth than another, but that also often depends on one's perspective—one's conditioning.

Although some conditioned ideas and beliefs appear to be truer and more helpful than others, it's not our business to try to change other people's conditioning unless they invite us to. Even when someone is our spouse, lover, parent, sibling, or close friend, changing their conditioning is still not our business.

Love Is More Important Than Conditioning

Not only is it not our business to change others, but it's also harmful to relationships to try to do so. Ideas are just not worth the price paid in love lost. Love is more important than any conditioned idea or belief, but if you take your conditioning more seriously than love, you will lose love. The other person will withhold love from you because it will be too painful for him or her to love you.

Conditioning takes this toll time and time again in relationships, and we assume the problem is a lack of love. Often, what causes relationships to break down or never leave the ground isn't a lack of love, but valuing ideas over love. When we are identified with the ego, we do choose ideas over love because being right is more important than loving. In the egoic state of consciousness, others' differences frighten us, and to feel safe, we feel we need to change them. So getting others to change seems very important.

In reality, love is always the safest choice, but the ego doesn't see this. Only Essence does, and we have to drop into Essence to realize this. Dropping into Essence isn't always easy to do in relationships because differences are so apparent and conditioning is triggered so frequently. Conditioning triggers judgment, and judgment triggers the desire to change someone, which causes conflict and pain and, consequently, withdrawal from relationship (i.e., the cold shoulder). For example, if your conditioning is that you like to be early for appointments and your partner's conditioning isn't the same, you are likely to say something unkind when your partner isn't ready when you are, if you are identified with your ego at the time. What you say is likely to be designed to punish or try to change your partner, which will be not only ineffective, but also destructive to the relationship.

The easiest place to stop this cycle is at the beginning, when the judgment first appears, because the judgment has the least momentum at that point. You can't keep judgments from arising because they aren't under your control or anyone else's, but *you can decide to do nothing about a judgment.* And that's the best choice you can make if you want love and relationship.

Many would argue that if someone doesn't conform to what they want, they don't want to be in that relationship anyway. That's their choice and the reason most relationships dissolve or never get started. Those who make this choice aren't likely to find love or a lasting and meaningful relationship with anyone because no one will ever meet their stiff and very personal requirements. Those who make this choice believe they will eventually meet someone who will meet all their criteria, so they keep looking and keep rejecting others. They explain their lack of relationship by saying that other people were too this or too that, but the question is, too this or that *for whom?* Who is it that has these requirements and preferences? It's the conditioned self—the ego—and it will never be pleased. As long as you let the ego choose your partners, you won't have one. The ego is in the business of rejecting others, not accepting and loving them.

For love, we need to turn to Essence because that's what knows how to love. When Essence is evoked in relationships, we find ourselves saying yes to love and no to our ideas about how others should be. We choose love instead of our conditioned preferences. Love feels too good to walk away from just because of some differences. The ego, on the other hand, prevents us from feeling love. It cuts love off with judgments before it even has a chance to be experienced. Those who are entrenched in the ego don't feel much love. Fortunately, love is less than a breath away, if only we turn our attention away from our judgments and onto the moment, which is full of exactly what we are looking for: love that is perfect just the way it is.

Noticing Love

When we want love on our own terms, we are unlikely to find it, or what we get is a person and relationship that matches our conditioning as much as possible. This kind of relationship isn't necessarily what will make us the happiest, however. The ego thinks it knows best about relationships and will settle for nothing less than what it wants. But what it wants is just not a good guide for happiness. What we want isn't always what will make us the happiest. *Following our desires is not the key to happiness.* It's what we think will make us happy, but it isn't what actually makes us happy.

Happiness lies in being aligned with Essence. When we are identified with Essence rather than with the ego, we have everything the ego is looking for, but pursuing in inept ways: happiness, joy, love, peace, and contentment. This is really everything you—and the ego—have ever wanted. It's just that the ego has a different way of trying to get these than Essence. From

Essence, *getting* is not required, only *being*. Happiness, joy, love, peace, and contentment are not arrived at by trying to get them, but by noticing that they are already here. Just check: Is love here now? Is happiness here now? Is peace here how? Is contentment here now? Noticing these qualities draws us into the experience of them.

To align yourself with Essence and experience love and the other qualities of Essence, all you have to do is notice love. When you *notice* love, you are, in a sense, *choosing* love over the ego's ideas, and that choice brings you into alignment with Essence. Essence lives for love and is not dissuaded from it by ideas or judgments or differences. It loves because it sees similarities, not differences. It sees how others are like itself—how others *are* itself. From Essence, you experience Oneness and unity with all life, and from this place, it is easy to love.

Taking Responsibility for Our Judgments

Judgments keep us under the ego's spell. The ego keeps us entranced with its ideas by making them seem important and by making the fulfillment of its desires seem necessary for happiness. It convinces us that what we think and desire are more important than they are. We think that to be happy, safe, and secure, we must have life and others match our ideas, and this just isn't true. However, as long as we believe this, either consciously or unconsciously, we will be under the ego's spell and we won't find happiness.

When we are identified with the ego, our ideas about how life and others should be seem really important. We are convinced that these ideas matter, and they don't. Does it really matter if your husband eats with his mouth open or your wife wears too much makeup? Does it really matter how much money your husband makes or how beautiful your wife is? It matters to your ego because you *think* these things make you look bad. You imagine all sorts of terrible things, particularly rejection by others, happening as a result. You give more importance to your fear of rejection than is reasonable. Rejection, to the ego, seems like a life-and-death matter, which it isn't, of course.

Notice how the ego is very uncomfortable with doing anything or having the partner do anything that doesn't match its conditioning. It gets

uncomfortable, scared, angry, ashamed, and embarrassed when you, or anyone who might reflect on you, break its conditioned rules about how to live.
An obvious example is how uncomfortable and scared you would feel if you
or your partner broke the law, when your conditioning is to be law abiding.
The same thing happens when you or your partner breaks one of your own
personal "laws" about how to behave in public or while eating or during sex
or while working or in any other circumstance, no matter how minor or
silly this "law" may seem to others. Here is an exercise to help you discover
the conditioning behind your judgments.

EXERCISE: EXAMINING THE CONDITIONING BEHIND JUDGMENT

The next time you feel an urge to judge your partner, examine the
conditioning that lies behind your judgment. Behind every judgment lies a "should" or a "should not." What "should" or "should not"
are you imposing on your partner? Notice how your judgment is
an attempt to get your partner to change his or her behavior so
that you don't have to feel uncomfortable.

When others do things we don't like because of our conditioning, we feel scared, angry, ashamed, or embarrassed. When you feel
these feelings, a judgment is probably not far behind. The judgment
that arises out of these feelings is an attempt to change the partner
and ease any discomfort. Watch this process. It's interesting to see
how predictable it is, and watching it is a good way to become more
aware of your own conditioning and to take responsibility for it.

It's not our partner's responsibility to change just because we have conditioning that demands that. Wanting our partner to change is not enough
reason for him or her to change, although the ego thinks it is and tries to manipulate by claiming, "If you loved me, you would change." If we want a loving relationship, we have to take responsibility for our conditioning and the
feelings generated by it, and choose to give up our judgments and attempts

to change our partner. When we do this, we discover true love because our partner will love us for being so loving, accepting, and allowing. There is nothing that opens someone's heart more than someone with an open heart. Conversely, there is nothing that closes someone's heart more than someone with a closed heart—and that means someone who is judging.

What to Do About Judgments

So what do you do when you feel like judging your partner? It's very tempting to indulge this impulse. First, you have to be convinced that judging isn't to your benefit, since the ego thinks it is. Are you convinced that love is more important than having your partner be the way you want him or her to be? Are you committed to love more than to your conditioning? The ego will opt out of relationship or try to change the relationship rather than choose love, but will you? Will you give in to the temptation to judge and remain separate, or will you choose love? It's up to you to make this choice whenever a judgment arises.

It's useful to see that the ego gets something from judging. It gets to feel superior, right, and separate. It takes pleasure in feeling this way. Notice that this pleasure is the payoff for judging. If there were no payoff, it would be easy to stop judging. Notice the self-righteousness and superiority you feel when you find something to criticize in someone. This is the payoff that is exchanged for love. Is it worth it? You need to decide because you can't have both.

Once you are convinced that love is worth passing up this payoff, you will have to catch the judgments before they are spoken. You will have to be aware enough to notice that conditioning has been triggered and that a choice needs to be made to give the conditioning your attention or not. If you give it your attention, the result will probably be a judgment. If you don't, the result will likely be love.

Even if you don't feel loving in the moment that you turn away from judging, your partner will appreciate your act of love, and your relationship will benefit from the accumulation of these small acts of love. In time, you will come to see how worthwhile it is to choose love instead of judgment, and doing this will become automatic. Here is an exercise that will help you become free of your judgments.

EXERCISE: PRACTICE LETTING JUDGMENTS BE

Practice just letting the judgment be there without doing any-thing about it. What's that like? This may feel uncomfortable and even unrewarding at first. Your ego will struggle and squirm and try to find a way around this. Eventually, letting judgments be will pay off in love, but you may need to just trust this at first while this habit becomes more established.

Notice what happens when you just let a judgment be there. Does the ego come in and try to talk you out of just letting it be? Does it offer a more concealed judgment or one that sounds a little nicer? Do feelings come up that create pressure to speak the judgment? What kinds of feelings most often arise? Can you just let them be there too without doing anything about them? They are also part of your conditioning.

Although you are responsible for what you do with your con-ditioning, you aren't responsible for the fact that it's there. It's just the programming you were given. Seeing this will help you de-tach from the conditioning and not act on it.

What if you send love to this conditioning and to the ego, which so desperately wants to act on it? Who is this *you* that is able to lovingly be with this conditioning? It's Essence, the *you* that is capable of love and a loving relationship.

Nothing is ever lost in choosing love. Your judgments never worked anyway. They only created anger, hurt, and separation. When you see the truth of this, it becomes much easier to choose love over judgment.

Honesty Is Not the Best Policy

Judgments aren't the only thing we shouldn't share with our partner. The ego's thoughts, in general, aren't necessarily useful to share. *Honesty is not the best policy, if that honesty comes from the ego.* In addition to judgments, the ego is full of opinions, complaints, and half-truths, and sharing these with our partner can only bring him or her into the egoic state of consciousness. And often, what the ego thinks is just plain hurtful. Most people are conditioned to believe that being honest is necessary and good for relationships when, in fact, it's often very detrimental. If being truthful means expressing the ego's truth, then it's better to not be truthful or to just keep quiet. The ego's truth is not the truth, and speaking it just keeps us identified with the ego and drags others into ego identification.

For instance, sharing what you don't like about your partner is just hurtful and doesn't serve. What's the point in telling your partner you don't like the way he or she smiles, or the way he or she dresses, or the way he or she drives, or the way he or she talks to the dog? It only creates tension between you. Sharing such information is generally an attempt, although an ineffective one, to change the other person to fit your preferences. If something you say will result in contraction rather than love, then it's better to not say it—even if it's true to you. Choose love rather than the ego's truth. The ego chooses to speak its truth instead of choosing to be loving because doing so gives it a feeling of being right. But the feeling of being right doesn't actually feel good, certainly not like love feels.

Even if your partner asks your opinion about how he or she looks, it never serves to be honest if you don't like something, especially if it isn't something that can be changed. It's one thing to say, "I like that dress better than the other one," and quite another to say, "I think you look a little fat in that." One expresses a preference about a dress, and the other expresses an opinion about the person's body, which can't easily be changed. Perhaps she says, "Do you think I've gained a little weight?" Even if you think she has, find a way to make her feel good instead of agreeing with her—for example, "You're as beautiful as ever!" Or if she says, "Are you mad at me?" you might say, "No, I'm mad about you." It feels good to say something nice, and the other person will appreciate your sweetness. You will have brought her into Essence and out of her critical mind. What a gift!

When the ego speaks, it results in contraction, bad feelings, and possibly tension and conflict in the relationship. When Essence speaks, on the other hand, people feel good, they relax, they feel love, and they give love. Paradise is restored! When Essence speaks, it expresses appreciation, approval, acceptance, compassion, patience, and love: "Take as much time as you want." "I love how you do that." "It's fine just the way it is." "It's not that easy to do." "You're so sweet." Essence compliments and uplifts rather than judges. This is the difference between heaven and hell on earth and in relationships.

Love is much more important than honesty. Honesty doesn't serve relationships when it creates contraction and tension. When contraction and tension are present, you can be sure that the ego's truth and not Essence's is being spoken. Let the results of your words be what determines whether you speak them or not. Speak only what brings harmony and love to the relationship and forgo what the ego has to say. That's a much better policy than honesty.

The Gift of Acceptance

Some people are easier to love than others, and they are the ones, therefore, who experience a lot of love. They experience it both within themselves and coming to them from others. What is their secret? Amazing good looks? No. Stunning personalities? No. Money and power? No. Their secret is none of the things we assume will make us more lovable. Their secret is that they love, and by that I mean, they accept others the way they are. Isn't that when you feel loved—when you feel accepted rather than judged, which is the usual way egos interact with each other?

Acceptance is the opposite of judgment and the antidote to it, and it brings us the experience of love. What is the experience of love? It is the experience of accepting and being accepted, the experience of relaxation, of being able to just be, without struggling and striving to be any different than we are or requiring that others be different than what they are. That is what we all want—to just be able to relax and be okay just the way we are and to be okay with others just the way they are.

When someone gives us this gift of acceptance, we love them. What a gift! It is a gift you would never reject and hopefully one you will return, because returning it—giving others this gift—brings you the experience of love. Loving and accepting others feels good. It is its own reward. It isn't even necessary for others to love and accept you in return because it's enough to just feel love and acceptance for others.

The ego loves, or tries to love, in order to get love or something else it wants. But this kind of love isn't really love. It's more like being nice, and it may not entail acceptance at all, but something more like tolerance for the purpose of getting something. This is a very different experience than love. Tolerating people is better than not tolerating them, but it's not the same as enjoying them, which can only come from true acceptance. You accept others because you appreciate the unique expression of life that they are. What amazing things these human forms are! And all the different personalities! When we can just let people be the way they are, it is such a relief—for us and for them. Allowing people to just *be* is loving them, and this appreciation and allowing comes from Essence. It is how Essence feels about life and every one of its creations.

What makes someone lovable? Certainly their acceptance of us makes them lovable. But what also makes them lovable is their acceptance of themselves. People who accept themselves, who are gentle and kind to themselves, are also gentle and kind to others. We see these qualities in them, and we relax. And when we relax, we return to Essence. People who love and accept themselves are lovable because they reflect Essence, and that's what we all really want—not someone to do our every bidding and match our every fantasy. What we really want is to be with someone who knows how to love because our deepest desire is to love. Therefore, we are drawn to those who know how to love. They are our teachers—the way-showers in this world. And this is our destiny as well—to be a place of refuge, where egos dissolve and all that is left is the love that we are.

SUMMARY

To help you choose love over judgment, remember:

1. Differences are not the problem they appear to be.

2. Judgments keep you identified with the ego.

3. It's not your business to change or improve your partner.

4. Your judgments are about you and are your responsibility.

5. Your ideas and desires are not as important as they seem.

6. Judgments prevent and kill love.

7. Judgments are ineffective at changing others.

8. Love is more important than ideas and beliefs.

9. You can't have both your judgments and love.

10. Don't be honest with your partner about what your ego thinks.

11. Give your partner the gift of acceptance. It's what you want too.

3

MOVING BEYOND ANGER

The Relationship Between Anger and Judgment

Like judgment, anger is an ongoing issue in most relationships because anger and judgment are closely related. They go hand in hand and often appear simultaneously. Anger both precedes and follows judgment: In the person who judges, anger precedes it so closely that they may seem simultaneous. In the person who receives the judgment, anger follows just as quickly and is likely to end in judging the judger. In one case, anger creates judgment, and in another case, judgment creates anger and more judgments.

If those involved aren't identified with the ego, there would be a different result. If someone is aligned with Essence when conditioning and feelings come up, then he or she will just notice the judgment and feelings and do nothing else about them, and that will be the end of it. Or if the recipient of anger and judgment remains identified with Essence and doesn't react to the anger and judgment, then that will be the end of it as well, because it's very difficult for someone delivering anger and judgment to remain in that state when the recipient doesn't join in. It takes two people identified with the ego to have a problem. If either one can remain identified with Essence, then anger and judgment will have no impact on the relationship.

For example, let's say your partner is angry because you forgot to pay a bill on time, and she says, "How could you have forgotten to do that? I even reminded you. Now we have a twenty-dollar late fee. What a waste of money! You just aren't careful with our money." (Notice how the ego takes a minor incident and spins it into a story of woe designed to shame the other person.) If you are able to stay in Essence and not take this personally and recognize that your partner is caught in fears and conditioning, your response might go something like this: "I'm really sorry I forgot that, honey. I'll try not to do that again." Pretty simple, isn't it? There's not much she can say to that! This response is likely to cause her to soften because you've just agreed with her rather than defending yourself. If you'd been identified with the ego, you probably would have tried to make yourself right or brought up a way she had been wrong in the past, even though you had clearly made a mistake in not paying that bill on time. Being right isn't worth it!

Remaining in Essence in the midst of or in the face of anger may be easier said than done, however. When someone's conditioning gets triggered in the context of relationship, usually the other's gets triggered too. That triggers even more conditioning, more anger, defensiveness, and blame, and the egos have their usual brawl, with no chance of reconciliation until someone's Essence steps in, which might not happen unless the participants take a break from each other. For the argument to subside, someone has to give up the fight. Only Essence does this. If Essence had entered the scene earlier, the disagreement wouldn't have escalated.

Conditioning provides the fuel for every disagreement. The ego actually likes a fight, and it will fight to make its point and get its way because how it feels and what it believes are important to it. The ego likes a fight because it's an opportunity to test its superiority and express its point of view, which it feels is the right one. This self-righteousness and sense of superiority fuel disagreements between egos. Both egos feel superior and self-righteous about their particular points of view. If the other were easily won over, there would never be a problem, but there are two egos in every relationship, and they behave similarly.

Having a point of view also gives the ego a sense that it exists. When it battles to get its point across, it is also battling to exist, in a sense, because without a point of view, the ego doesn't exist. *After all, what else is the ego but a point of view?* The ego is the sense of being separate, and having a point of view gives it a sense of separateness and individuality.

Our particular point of view comes from our conditioning, which is composed of rules, "shoulds," beliefs, opinions, and other ideas. In relationships, this conditioning gets expressed in judgments, which are often stated as conclusions about someone (e.g., "You are selfish") and designed to explain why someone doesn't comply with the wishes and demands that are part of our conditioning. These conclusions are not facts, but our point of view. They are stories we make up about someone. Anger and self-righteousness (the conviction that we are right) fuel these judgments and provide us with the energy to fight over them.

Here is how anger and judgment cause differences in conditioning to get out of hand: Conditioning comes up with a statement such as, "He shouldn't leave his dishes in the sink." (Watch out for those "should" statements!) Then anger and self-righteousness come up around this statement, and you form a judgment (conclusion) about the other: "You're a slob" or "You're inconsiderate" or "You're lazy," depending on your current perspective. Telling this story makes you even angrier. Then you search your memory for other incidents to support your claim, and you get even angrier. Now you're so angry you can't contain your anger, and you have to tell your partner what you think of him. What you say next doesn't have much to do with the dishes in the sink. All of this can happen in seconds.

Differences in conditioning are not really that hard to deal with, but the feelings and stories that surround these issues can be. These feelings and stories come from a very irrational part of ourselves—the ego—which doesn't care as much about the truth as being right. It will say anything to defend its point of view because being wrong and backing off is the last thing it wants. For the ego to give up its point of view is to admit defeat, and the ego doesn't do that without a fight. It has its pride, after all.

Pride is another problem in relationships. Pride, like judgment, is another way we keep ourselves separate from and superior to others. We imagine that we are better than them, and that evokes pride. This is not the pride in a job well done, but a negative kind of pride—one that takes pleasure in diminishing others because that makes the ego feel superior. The pride of the ego is not a pretty thing, and when it shows up in relationships, conflict isn't far behind. It's part of many incidents that involve anger and judgment.

When we feel angry in the context of relationship, it's a sign that our conditioning has been triggered and is causing our ego to take a fighting stance. One of the favorite ways the ego fights is with judgments. It hurls names, blame, criticism, and other disparaging remarks at the person who's responsible for triggering the conditioning. The person who triggers our conditioning, which is often our partner, is blamed for the fact that we feel angry, but it isn't that person's fault. No one is to blame for our anger, but to the ego it feels like someone did something that shouldn't have been done.

What Not to Do with Anger

Once anger is there, you can't make it go away. You are stuck with it, but only momentarily if you know how to handle it. If you don't feed it by telling a story, it will just disappear. Anger gets out of hand because we try to support and defend it with a story. We feel uncomfortable about being angry, so we make up a story to justify our anger, and this story intensifies our feelings. This story often has little to do with the conditioning that triggered the anger.

For example, you hear kids making noise as they play outside in the street, and this triggers your conditioning: "Kids shouldn't play in the street." (Another "should" statement.) This view seems true to you, although many kids and even their parents would disagree, so you feel angry and self-righteous. However, the amount of anger you feel seems out of proportion to the situation, so you have to tell a story to justify the intensity of your feelings: "Last year, when they played ball in the street, they broke the Smiths' window." The trouble is that telling this story makes you feel even angrier and more justified in your anger. You stew about this story a little longer and come up with a few more reasons why kids shouldn't play in the street. Your mind searches for examples in the past and reaches for reasons why kids playing in the street would be bad in the future, and you conclude something out of proportion to the original thought: "I've got to move out of this neighborhood!" Now kids are to blame for your having to move. Anger—or really the stories we tell and the conclusions we come to—causes us a lot of trouble, and this is doubly true in relationships.

Telling stories to justify your anger and drumming up more reasons to be angry is definitely not the way to deal with anger, unless you like being angry and fighting. But it does give the ego some degree of pleasure, which is why we do it.

EXERCISE: NOTICING HOW THE EGO ENJOYS FINDING FAULT

It's useful to notice the enjoyment the ego gets from finding fault and picking a fight. Most of all, it's useful to notice that it is the ego that is doing this, and you are not the ego. That means you don't have to find fault. Doing so is a choice, and you can choose to do something else.

Whether you are telling stories to justify the anger, drumming up more reasons to be angry, going back over past incidents that made you angry, or thinking about what might make you angry in the future, thinking about anything related to the conditioning and the anger is just not helpful. Nevertheless, this is exactly what the ego does. As a way of sustaining the conditioning, the ego often mentally repeats it: "You shouldn't leave your dishes in the sink. You just shouldn't do it. How can someone do that? It's just not right." In the same way, the ego sustains the anger by repeatedly going over its stories about it and justifications for it: "He's an inconsiderate slob. He's always been a slob. His mother was a slob. I would never do that to him. He just doesn't care about me. Maybe he never cared. I don't think he loves me. He's too much of a slob for me. He's not considerate enough for me. Maybe I don't love him." In a few short minutes, the internal dialogue has gone from being annoyed at dishes in the sink to considering divorce. Anger causes us to lose touch with our love for someone. It also kills the desire for sex with that person.

Thinking is what holds the ego in place and keeps the conditioning, feelings, and unhappiness going. It creates and maintains problems. It's a real troublemaker. Choosing to believe thoughts is choosing to be identified with the ego, and it's possible to make another choice.

Another thing that doesn't help in dealing with anger is blaming yourself for it or for the conditioning that caused it. Taking anger personally (by assuming blame for it) makes you feel bad about yourself and will only take you deeper into the anger because you'll feel like you have to justify it. And justifying your anger will only create more anger and more bad feelings about yourself.

You don't need to justify your anger or defend your conditioning because they are not yours. They don't belong to you—to the real you—but to the false self. You are only responsible for what you do with them once they are there.

Just as it's not helpful to blame yourself for the anger, it's not helpful to blame others for it either. The ego's strategy for feeling better about being angry is to make up stories to justify it and to blame others for it. This just creates more anger and bad feelings all around. By blaming someone else, we involve another person, who also has an ego and its own conditioning, judgments, and bad feelings. And that's just more trouble.

Contrary to common belief, it is also not helpful to share your anger with your partner. The general assumption about anger is that if we don't do something about it or talk about it, we aren't dealing with it. But, unfortunately, most of what we say or do about our anger is destructive to relationships. You may think that telling your partner when you're angry is healthy, but that's a misconception. It's far better to notice the anger, take responsibility for it, and not dump it on, or even try to process it with, your partner, because doing so doesn't serve the anger or the relationship.

Here's an example of what might happen when you tell your partner you are angry at her for throwing out something you needed. You might say something like this:

> I can't believe you threw out that paper. Now I don't know who to call about this. You always do that. I wish you wouldn't straighten up my desk and papers. You could at least ask me before throwing something away. You're so compulsive. You really need to look at that.

This may seem like a perfectly reasonable response to this situation. However, the truth is that the paper is gone, and any discussion about it isn't going to change that. And your partner's future behavior isn't likely to change either if you alienate her by criticizing her. More likely, it will trigger her ego and anger in an attempt to defend herself:

> I just couldn't stand the mess anymore. You should clean up your desk. You know it bothers me when it's messy. I can't help it. I needed to clean under those papers. If

I left it up to you, it would be filthy in here—and you wouldn't even care!

At this point, she's not any closer to cooperating with you in the future, and now you both feel angry. And nothing has changed. The paper is still gone. Is your anger worth it? Is being right worth it? Is punishing each other with angry words worth it?

Keeping the anger to yourself is not the same thing as repressing it, which is denying that it's there or being completely unaware that it's there. You acknowledge that it's there, but you keep it to yourself. The reason for this advice is twofold: First, by keeping it to yourself, you are not as likely to dwell on it and feed it with stories to try to convince your partner of your position. Second, by keeping it to yourself, you avoid the possibility of triggering your partner's conditioning and a potentially unproductive or destructive interaction.

Discussions about conditioning aren't helpful if you and your partner are identified with the ego because they're bound to turn into arguments, which are destructive to a relationship. From this level, little can be accomplished. In discussing conditioning with your partner, the best that can be hoped for is that you come to understand each other's conditioning, but unless you both are identified with Essence when you are doing it, exploring conditioning isn't likely to be productive.

Even this approach has its limitations and dangers. Although your intent may be to explore and understand conditioning and not blame or judge your partner, your conditioning may get triggered by this discussion, and it may turn into an argument or at least become unproductive. There's also no guarantee that the insights you come up with will be that useful or applied when the going gets tough. These insights can just as easily be discovered independently of each other by meditating on the issue and asking for internal guidance. You don't need to get insight about your conditioning or your partner's from your partner. You can get it from yourself, and it's much safer to get it that way.

The same is true about processing your conditioning. If this is done at all, it's better to do it by yourself than with your partner, who has his or her own issues and points of view, which may not be that helpful to your understanding and healing. A therapist may be valuable, but don't make the mistake of thinking that your partner can or should be your therapist. The ego is very tricky, and even couples with very pure intentions, a good grasp of psychology, and good communication skills can get sidetracked into blame, judgment, anger, and irrationality because the ego can be triggered at any time.

How Not to Feed Anger

The best way to disarm anger so that it doesn't become a destructive force in your relationships is to not give it any attention. Instead, just notice it and do nothing else about it. It can help to remind yourself that the anger is just conditioning arising and that, as such, it's not worth paying attention to. By sending the opposite message, the egoic mind keeps us involved with anger. It convinces us that the anger we are feeling is important, meaningful, true, and must be expressed. Because of the tendency to believe this, you may have established a habit of expressing anger. In that case, you may need to counteract this habit with affirmations that have the opposite effect—ones that make it easier to put your attention elsewhere, for example: "It's just conditioning" or "Love is more important than this."

One thing that can help you ignore your anger and the conditioning behind it is to pay attention to something else. When you're told not to think of a pink elephant, of course, pink elephants are all you can think about. Likewise, if you try to not pay attention to the anger and the thoughts behind it, you are likely to pay attention to them. Paying attention to anything else will get your mind off the conditioning and anger. Thinking gives the anger fuel, and if you cut off the fuel, the anger will dissipate. However, you have to cut off the fuel for long enough and continue to do so every time the anger returns.

Some conditioning is very persistent, especially if you've habitually indulged the anger. The egoic mind will try to overwhelm you with thoughts and reasons why the anger should be expressed, and these can be difficult to ignore. Through persistence, the ego is often able to erode our best intentions to ignore the anger. The conditioning behind very compelling thoughts and feelings might need to be addressed through closer examination or therapy before the thoughts and feelings become less compelling. Nevertheless, doing your best to repeatedly put your attention elsewhere and not indulge the anger will be rewarded by an eventual lessening of the power of the thoughts and the anger.

There are a number of things you can put your attention on instead. For one, you can put it on a more positive thought. However, giving attention to any kind of thought is a little tricky because it keeps you involved with the mind, and the next thing you know, you're paying attention to a negative thought again.

A much better strategy is to turn your awareness away from the world of thought to the real world—to what's happening right now, in the present moment. One way to focus on the moment is to pay attention to what is coming in through your senses. When you do this, be sure you pay attention to the experience of seeing, listening, and sensing and not to any thoughts about the experience. It's easy to get ambushed by the mind. If this happens, just bring yourself back to the *experience* of seeing, listening, and sensing.

Paying attention to the senses takes you out of your mind and into your body and the moment. Experiencing your body brings you into the moment, which is the domain of Essence and where true happiness is found. The mind holds us hostage, in its world of struggle and pain. It convinces us that we need to be in the world of thought, the world of the past and the future. We are programmed to believe its version of life and how to be happy, but when we drop into the moment and into Essence we discover something else—our real Self!

Many other things can bring us into the moment as well, and these things are covered more extensively in other books of mine. Beauty is one of the things that brings us into the moment. Seeing something beautiful, particularly something in nature, can drop us into Essence, where the insignificance and untruth of our conditioning is obvious. When we are experiencing Essence, our conditioned ideas are put in perspective and seen for what they are—programming. It's obvious they have nothing to do with who we really are. When we are aligned with Essence, we are aware of the thoughts in our mind, but we understand they have nothing to do with who we really are. We know they are part of the conditioned self—the false self.

Focusing on, or paying attention to, anything other than our thoughts brings us into the moment and into the experience of Essence. When our mind is focused on something, it's not thinking, but experiencing what it's focused on. For example, if you focus on your breath, you're noticing the experience of breathing. Or if you focus on what you're doing, you're notic-ing the experience of doing.

Focusing on anything or just noticing what is happening now in this moment automatically brings us into the moment and aligns us with Essence simply because when we are focusing or noticing, we aren't think-ing. If you want to go back to the ego's world, just start thinking again: start thinking about what breathing means or tell a story about why you're doing what you're doing instead of just experiencing these things, and you'll be back in the mind. And your next thought is likely to be a con-ditioned one.

EXERCISE: NOT FEEDING THE ANGER

The next time you feel angry, notice what went on just before you felt angry. What thought caused you to feel angry? Where did this thought come from? It just arose out of nowhere. That is conditioning. You didn't invite that thought, and you didn't create it; it just appeared. The anger appeared out of nowhere too. You can't do anything about this thought or the anger, but you can do something about what happens next. And what you choose to do at this point is crucial.

Stop the cycle of anger right away by not feeding it with more thoughts (stories) and feelings. If you don't give your attention to thoughts related to the conditioning and the anger, the anger will subside. Withdraw your attention from those thoughts and the anger, and put it on something else. This isn't denial or repres-sion, but good mental health. You replace a habit that's mentally unhealthy with a healthy one.

Although you can't prevent conditioned thoughts and an-ger from arising, by turning your attention to something positive or beautiful (something of Essence), and bringing yourself into the moment by focusing on experience rather than on thought, you drop into Essence, where the anger and conditioning aren't a problem.

How to Work with Anger

There are times when it's beneficial to examine the conditioning that is the source of our anger. When the same conditioning and anger come up repeatedly and compellingly, something about it may need to be seen before it becomes weak enough to stop hooking us. We all have conditioning that's difficult to ignore—issues that come up again and again and never seem to get resolved. These issues affect our relationships, as we go round and round with our partner in an attempt to resolve them.

Relationships are no place to resolve our personal issues. They certainly trigger those issues, but that's exactly why they aren't the place to work on these things. Besides the fact that your partner is probably not a therapist, it's not your partner's responsibility to heal you. It's yours. Fortunately, it's possible to work through many of our issues on our own. For the ones that are driven by repressed emotions and other deep-seated complexes, psychotherapy, hypnotherapy, or some other healing modality is recommended.

There's a way to diminish the compelling nature of conditioning. Becoming aware of what you are thinking and feeling is the key. To do this, you have to move from being absorbed in thinking and feeling to witnessing your thoughts and feelings. From this more objective place, you can notice and contemplate your thoughts.

The egoic mind is the ego-driven and ego-controlled mind. When the mind is under the control of the ego, it's irrational and compulsively driven by conditioning and the ego's goals. Fortunately, the mind is also capable of being used by Essence, which uses the mind to break through the spell cast by the ego. It does this by introducing objectivity and analysis to the irrationality of the egoic mind. Essence uses the mind to unravel conditioning and diminish the power of the ego. Essence's ability to do this is what makes it possible for us to wake up out of the illusion of being separate and realize our true nature as Oneness.

To get free of our most compelling conditioning, we need to enlist Essence's help by aligning with the aspect of the mind that is capable of witnessing and analyzing our thoughts. We actually observe and examine our thoughts all the time, but when deep-seated complexes or other entrenched conditioning comes up, we often lose our ability to witness and analyze our thoughts and feelings. We "go unconscious" and just react to them. When this is happening, we need to learn to notice that, and noticing that will reestablish ourselves as the Witness. This isn't as difficult as it may sound because it's easy enough to tell when we are reacting unconsciously; but often at that point we don't care what's happening because we are so involved in our feelings.

The most obvious sign of going unconscious is feeling angry. Other strong feelings are signs as well, but anger is an especially obvious sign because it manifests so noticeably in the body. When you feel angry, you've bought into some idea long enough to trigger your emotions. This happens almost instantly, but the anger will only grow and be sustained if you heap more ideas onto the initial idea. Once that happens, to dissipate the anger, you will need to become aware of the initial idea and the others too.

Anger is a sign that you need to do some inquiry to trace back and uncover the ideas that created and fueled the anger. Inquiry is a matter of asking some very simple questions: What triggered the anger? What "should," unmet expectation, or other belief is behind it? Is that true? Keep asking these questions until you have uncovered some of the untrue beliefs behind your anger. When you see their untruth, their ability to cause you to become angry is lessened.

For example, you are really angry that your partner is having an affair with someone. Most people would agree that you should be angry and he or she deserves any fallout that may occur. But that's the ego talking. Anger doesn't feel good, and you don't have to carry it around with you. It's damaging to your health, to your relationships, and potentially to every area of your life. Anger doesn't serve, so it serves you to not let it take over, even when it seems justified. Of course, anger would arise in this situation, but it will only continue if you dwell on this feeling and the thoughts that caused it.

What thoughts might be behind this anger and the hurt that is undoubtedly there too? There are probably many. When you look, you discover the following negative conclusions, or stories, you've spun about the affair: "He never loved me. I'm not beautiful enough. I'll never find someone like him again. No one will ever love me. I can't live without him. I hate him. He shouldn't have done that." Those are sweeping statements, and none of them are true, no matter how true they may feel in the moment. *The strength of our feelings is not an indication of truth, but of how much power we have given the thoughts behind the feelings—how much we have believed these thoughts and how often we have thought them.*

Essence is able to bring objectivity, equanimity, and peace to even this situation if we are willing to experience the truth of this situation rather than the ego's stories about it. Essence's truth is that even this experience serves in some way, and Essence will show you how it serves and how to deal with it if you listen to your Heart rather than to your egoic mind. It is all good, and when you drop into your Heart, you know this.

Here is an inquiry you can do when you feel angry.

INQUIRY: DISCOVERING WHAT IS BEHIND YOUR ANGER

Ideas that trigger anger are most often "shoulds" and unmet expectations. The next time you feel angry, look for the reason. What triggered the anger? Was it something someone did or said? Most conditioning is triggered by things others say and do, and the tendency is to blame others for how we feel.

Rather than blaming others, get curious about what your anger stems from. Finding the stimulus is only the beginning because that stimulus isn't the cause of your anger. The real cause is what you told yourself as a result of that stimulus. Sometimes these thoughts are so quick or unconscious we aren't even aware of thinking them. Look and see what really caused you to be angry. Look for a belief about how things should be and how they don't meet this expectation.

Once you find the "should" or unmet expectation behind your anger, ask, "Is that true?" "Shoulds" are programmed ideas about the way life is supposed to be. They are always false because life is the way it is, and any attachment to life being different from that is the cause of your unhappiness. Keep examining the answers your mind comes up with to explain why things should be the way you think they should be. Keep asking, "Is that true?" You are likely to uncover many lies (partial truths) that are fueling your anger, both consciously and unconsciously.

This kind of inquiry is very beneficial because it unmasks the egoic mind's lies, and once they are unmasked, they lose their power. However, these lies may need to be unmasked many times before they stop arising, but each time you do so, they become weaker. Freeing yourself from conditioning takes commitment and persistence, and the ego will try to talk you out of it by telling you this inquiry doesn't help. If you really want to be free, you won't listen.

Sometimes feelings are so strong that you can't take your mind off of them and put it on something else. They may even be so strong that you find it difficult to do inquiry. When that happens, the best way to work with your anger is to just be there with it, without trying to change it or doing anything about it. Just sit with it on an energetic level and see what happens.

EXERCISE: BEING WITH THE ANGER

When your anger is especially strong, try just letting it be there without turning your attention elsewhere, moving away from the anger, expressing it, trying to change it, or even inquiring into what caused it. Just be with the energy of it. What is the experience of it energetically? How would you describe it? How big is it? What color is it? How does it feel? Where is it? Allow the energy to be just as it is and notice if it changes as you do this. What happens to it? Is there really anything you need to do about it?

Anger scares us and makes us uncomfortable, so we tend to do something to try to make it go away. We dump it onto others and make them deal with it. Trying to get rid of our anger by involving others leaves everyone feeling worse. When we just let it be there, it eventually dissolves back into the emptiness from which it came.

What Drives Anger

The thoughts that underlie and fuel anger are nearly always about unmet needs and desires: you want something, and you don't have it, and that

SUMMARY: WHAT TO DO WITH ANGER

1. Don't blame yourself for your anger or for the conditioning that caused it.

2. Don't blame others for your anger.

3. Don't talk about the anger or try to process it with your partner.

4. Don't keep thinking about what made you angry.

5. Don't try to explain or justify your anger with stories.

6. Remind yourself that anger is just a sign that conditioning is arising and you don't need to do anything about it.

7. Give your attention to something else: positive thoughts, sounds, beauty, sensations, your breath, or what you're doing.

8. Be present to the experience of the moment.

9. When anger comes up repeatedly, uncover, through inquiry, the complex of thoughts that drive the anger. What "shoulds," expectations, or other beliefs are behind it? Are they true?

10. When anger is very strong, be very present to it. Be with it energetically without expressing it, thinking about it, or trying to change it, and see what happens.

makes you angry. The problem isn't really the unmet needs and desires, but rather what we tell ourselves about them. The egoic mind convinces us that they are the cause of our unhappiness and if they were met, we would be happy. This is the biggest of the lies underpinning our anger. Our happiness is not dependent on our needs and desires being met, but if we believe that, it's just as good as true because believing that causes us to be unhappy.

For example, let's suppose you want to own a house. It's absolutely possible for someone to be happy without owning a house. There's plenty of evidence for this. Nevertheless, you say to yourself: "All of my friends have houses. Why can't I have a house? I should own a house by this time in my life. How can I have a social life if I don't own a house? I'll never be happy until I own a house." This is quite a string of assumptions, and each one is untrue. Believing these untruths has the potential to make you feel very bad—and angry. Let's look at each statement more closely:

1. "All of my friends have houses" carries the implication that there's something wrong with you for not owning a house. Believing this will make you feel bad about yourself and your life.

2. "Why can't I have a house?" implies entitlement, as if it's unfair that you don't own a house. The expectation that you should have a house, while you don't actually have one, is likely to make you feel angry.

3. "I should own a house by this time in my life." Is that true? No. There are no rules about this except the ones you create and then suffer over. Believing this will result in feelings of shame and inferiority, and those feelings can lead to anger and resentment toward others who have what you don't have.

4. "How can I have a social life if I don't own a house?" This is another false assumption. It assumes you will be unpopular or unloved if you don't own a house. This gives owning a house more importance than it actually deserves. If you believe this, you will feel sad and angry.

5. "I'll never be happy until I own a house." This conclusion is based on the previous statements. You built a case that convinced you that you can't be happy until you own a house. This belief justifies the feelings the other statements generated: you have good reason to be angry about not owning a house—because you'll never be happy until you do.

If you believe the lies the egoic mind tells you about what you need to be happy, you will never be happy. Not only that, you will probably be very angry at life, at God, and at others, including your partner, when you don't get what you want. The egoic mind drums up desires and convinces us that we need what we desire to be happy. When we don't get that, we feel angry. Anger comes from the misunderstanding that we need to have our desires met to be happy.

Desires don't have anything to do with happiness (although they have a lot to do with unhappiness). Ask anyone who has had lots of desires met. And check this out for yourself: Has fulfilling your desires brought anything but a very fleeting *feeling* of happiness? Has this feeling ever been enough? There's another kind of happiness that is deeper, more satisfying, and ever present, and it's not dependent on getting or having anything. It's dependent on just being.

For the egoic mind, there's a fine line between needs and desires. To the ego, desires *are* needs. It doesn't see that desires are just thoughts and that there are actually very few real needs. Even so, these real needs don't have to be met for us to be happy. Even basic needs, such as food, water, shelter, and warmth, have little to do with actual happiness. Just ask the many ascetics in India, who find happiness in just being alive and who find happiness even in dying. Even unmet needs are not the cause of unhappiness; the cause of unhappiness is what we *tell ourselves* about not having them met.

Desires in the Context of a Relationship

Desires are thoughts (often with feelings attached to them), and as such belong to the egoic mind. Whenever you want something, it's most likely coming from your conditioning. Can you think of anything you want that isn't something your ego wants? Even wanting spiritual liberation or to be free of conditioning comes from the ego, because Essence doesn't want. The feeling of wanting comes from the ego, not Essence. Essence has intentions and produces drives within us, but it doesn't want. All thoughts that begin with "I want" come from the ego because its job is to generate desires. That's how it motivates us to do what it envisions for our life. The ego has an agenda, and it carries out and fuels that agenda with desires and other ideas.

We think our desires, just like our other thoughts, are meaningful and important when, in fact, they often cause us to pursue things that aren't meaningful and fulfilling at all. Desires are very poor guides for how to live our life.

If there weren't an alternative, we would be in trouble. But Essence also has an agenda, a plan, and it motivates us through our intuition and through spontaneous urges to act. Life can and does unfold very nicely from Essence when we are aligned with it. Our desires, however, keep us identified with the ego and doing its bidding rather than Essence's.

It's ironic that so many arguments in relationships are caused by a conflict of desires, because desires are really not worth fighting over. For example, if you want to go on a trip and your partner wants to spend that money on a new sofa, or if you want a traditional wedding and your fiancé wants to elope, are those desires more important than love—more important than your relationship? Desires are conditioning, and conditioning is not more important than love. When you drop into Essence, you know this. Arguing doesn't happen when both people are in Essence because there's nothing to argue about. Negotiation can certainly happen, though. From Essence, conditioning is just conditioning; it's nothing more than an idea, and how much substance and importance is there in an idea? Essence's point of view is that no idea is worth losing love over.

Nevertheless, desires come up as much when we are in relationship as they do when we are single. However, they are more of a problem in relationship because they are bound to conflict with your partner's, at least some of the time. At least when you are single, you are responsible for your own desires: a desire is generated, you pursue it, and if it doesn't work out, you get angry and blame yourself. Something very different happens in relationships: a desire is generated, you discuss it with your partner, you pursue it, and if it doesn't work out, you get angry and blame your *partner*.

In relationships, desires are the cause of much blame. But that's true of all conditioning: When you feel angry, you blame your partner. When you feel sad or depressed, you blame your partner. When judgments get stirred up, you blame your partner. When your ideas don't work out, you may even find a way to blame your partner for that. The ego doesn't take responsibility for its wrong thinking and bad decisions, and it doesn't like being wrong. So it tries to make someone else wrong. Our partner is a very convenient scapegoat.

We expect so much from our partner and our relationship. We have so many desires and expectations tied to relationship that it's no wonder we get angry at our partner as much as we do. If unfulfilled expectations and desires create anger (and they do), then we are going to be angry a lot in relationships because we have so many expectations and desires related not only to our partner, but also to relationship in general. We have lots and lots of ideas, including desires, when it comes to relationship. We really do hope (and expect) that our partner will fulfill our desires as a mate and give us the kind of relationship we want. But, as we will see, that's an impossible task.

4

MOVING BEYOND
ROMANTIC ILLUSIONS

The Levels of a Relationship

Every couple relates on two different levels of consciousness: the level of the ego and the level of Essence. In any moment, either level is possible, and one of these always predominates because these levels are mutually exclusive—that is, we can't relate from the ego and from Essence at the same time, although we can move very quickly from one to the other. Just as with individual consciousness, the levels of relating can change rapidly back and forth between ego and Essence.

The level two people relate from as a couple depends on what level they spend most of their time at as individuals: If they are identified with the ego most of the time, then their relating as a couple will primarily be from the ego. Similarly, if they are identified with Essence most of the time, then their relating as a couple will be primarily from there.

Most couples who get along well are at a similar level of consciousness—that is, they spend a similar amount of time identified with ego and with Essence. Those who are at very different levels of consciousness have much more difficulty getting along and therefore are less likely to stay together. Although this is only one factor in compatibility, it's one of the most important ones. Without this similarity, a relationship is unlikely to be very fulfilling, and most wouldn't even get started. (The exception to this truth is karmic relationships, which are often between people of different levels of consciousness. Although difficult because of these differences, karmic relationships are fulfilling in their own way and often endure despite the difficulties because they serve a spiritual purpose.)

When two people are at different levels of consciousness, each unconsciously tries to get the other to relate at his or her level, which creates an ongoing sense of struggle. The person who is more identified with Essence can grow resentful of being drawn back into ego identification when that happens, while the one who is more identified with the ego resists experiencing Essence because that's what egos do. That person may enjoy being in Essence once he or she experiences it, but that doesn't change the fact it was a struggle to get there.

The Role of the Personality in Relationships

As for the personality, that is the vehicle through which the relating happens: either the ego uses the personality or Essence does. When the ego operates through the personality, the expression is more selfish and less likable than when Essence does, because Essence expresses the personality in the most positive way possible, although the characteristics of the personality remain the same.

For instance, if someone's personality is outgoing and independent, then that remains true whether the ego or Essence is expressing itself through the personality. When the ego expresses itself through such a personality, the outgoingness might be over the top or used to manipulate others through flattery and charm. Similarly, the independence might lean toward willfulness or lack of compromise. On the other hand, when Essence expresses these same qualities, the outgoingness would be sincerely charming and personable. The independence would manifest as a healthy independence that takes into account the needs and feelings of others.

We are often attracted to those with opposite qualities because they fascinate us, and often we need to develop the qualities they so naturally express; however, we like those who have similar personalities to ours. So while we are attracted to opposites, we feel most comfortable and at home with those who are like us.

The ego doesn't like differences, but Essence finds them stimulating, interesting, and beneficial to our growth, so it often draws to us those who are different. Nevertheless, those Essence intends for us to be with long term tend to be more similar to us. This similarity makes it easier for us to get along with them day to day because conditioning is an issue in every relationship, and it's triggered less between those who are more similar.

Factors in Compatibility

The personality is not as important in relationships as we tend to think. There are many people you are compatible with on a personality level, but who you would have no interest in being with. For a good relationship, much more is needed than similar or compatible personalities.

Similar soul age, which relates to the level of consciousness, is very important to compatibility because it accounts for similar lessons, values, and life goals and for seeing the world similarly. The person you are likely to be the happiest and most fulfilled with is undoubtedly someone of a similar soul age.

Spiritual compatibility is much more important to success and happiness in relationships than personality compatibility. Spiritual compatibility includes not only a similar level of consciousness and soul age, but also compatible, similar, or related life purposes or lessons. A connection with someone who is destined to be part of what we came into life to accomplish or learn is a much more powerful connection than with someone with whom we have only compatible personalities or even soul ages. Nevertheless, before coming into life, we often choose a personality that will be compatible with those who are important to our life purpose and lessons, because there's some value in that compatibility.

Similar personalities smooth the way for relating because less conditioning is triggered when there are fewer differences. And yet people can have similar personalities and still have very different conditioning because of different backgrounds or cultures. Similarity in backgrounds is extremely important to compatibility for the same reason that other similarities are: getting along with someone who has very different conditioning can be very challenging. Sometimes, however, this challenge is part of our lessons or life purpose. In that case, the differences are likely to be experienced as interesting and felt to give meaning to the relationship.

Although physical attraction seems very important to compatibility, even more important perhaps than personality, over time it becomes much less important than other factors that lend longevity and meaning to a relationship. Physical attraction is not as big a component in sexual compatibility and happiness as you might think. If spiritual compatibility and other factors that create harmony are there, a couple can have a very happy life, including a happy sex life, with a minimum of physical attraction.

There is one catch, however: If the couple isn't relating from Essence, a lack of physical attraction may be too much of a barrier to overcome. Physical attraction is more of a must in relationships where the individuals are identified with the ego, especially in this culture. It's less important in relationships where the individuals are identified with Essence, especially when there's a common life purpose or lesson. The reason physical attraction seems so important is because most people are identified with the

SUMMARY: COMPATIBILITY FACTORS
(in order of importance)

1. Of greatest importance are compatible, similar, or related life purposes.

2. Similar soul age is another strong foundational factor.

3. Similar conditioning as a result of similar backgrounds and cultures also contributes to harmony and longevity; however, differences may stretch us in ways we need to be stretched, which can be fulfilling.

4. Similar personalities contribute to friendship and day-to-day harmony, but some differences make a relationship interesting and stimulating and lead to growth.

5. Physical attraction is one of the most compelling factors initially, but if the other factors aren't there, it won't mean much over time.

ego most of the time. So without physical attraction, many relationships wouldn't even get started. However, physical attraction is actually more of a minor ingredient in the recipe of love; we can do all right without it, and other things can substitute for it. Lack of physical attraction can still be a challenge for a couple, but if their relationship serves a spiritual purpose, it's probably one they are willing to deal with.

Friendship Within a Romantic Relationship

The love that exists for a friend is no less important or meaningful than the love that exists for a lover. It's very similar and equally valuable. It's often easier to relate from Essence with a friend than with a lover because we generally bring fewer expectations to our friendships than we do to our romantic relationships. Expectations of our lover, which involve "shoulds," desires, and demands, keep us tied to the ego and relating from it.

Another reason it's easier to relate from Essence with a friend is that we are less identified with our friends than with our lovers, so we place fewer demands on them to be a certain way. It's easier to let our friends be the way they are. The ego sees the lover as a reflection of itself and attempts to shape him or her into a worthy reflection. The ego also has lots of ideas about what a lover should be like and fewer ideas about a friend, and the ones it does have of a friend are less charged and held more lightly.

One of the things that makes friendship possible within a romantic relationship is a similar kind of lightness and acceptance of the partner. Couples who are also friends let each other be the way they are. They may do this, in part, because compatibility on a number of levels means they just happen to like and approve of each other. For whatever reason, they are able to accept each other and let each other be. They may even find the partner's conditioning endearing.

Friends accept each other, either because they are similar or have similar interests, or because they just choose to accept each other. It's possible to be friends with or to love anyone if we are willing to accept that person. Acceptance *is* love: We accept those we love, and we love those we accept. Acceptance is a choice, which means that love is a choice.

Love Is a Choice

We tend to think of love as an uncontrollable feeling that comes over us. Although this overwhelming feeling does happen, real love and love that is sustained is always a choice: you choose to be open to someone, you choose to accept them, and that openness and acceptance allows love to flow. This process is often unconscious, so we often don't realize we are choosing to accept someone when it's happening. But that choice to accept someone is what precedes love. It happens unconsciously all the time, and it can happen more consciously too.

When acceptance and love happen unconsciously, it's often because someone fits our ideas, desires, and conditioning. We find that person pleasing because we identify with him or her in some way, probably because we see qualities similar to ours, or perhaps because we see a quality we admire and would like to develop. When our acceptance doesn't happen automatically and unconsciously, we can simply choose to accept someone *because* he or she is different or unusual in some way.

You can learn to welcome and embrace differences rather than reject them, as the ego does. When you do that, you open up a new world of possibilities in relationship with people you never thought you could love. You still might not choose to have relationships with them, but you don't have to miss out on the experience of love by rejecting them just because they're different from you or because they don't match your conditioning in some other way.

It's useful to notice how much you withhold love from others because they are different. Once you become more conscious of this tendency, you are free to make another choice—to choose to celebrate differences rather than reject them—and that choice opens your heart and your life up to new possibilities.

The Role of Conditioning in Relationships

Conditioning and the ego are what stand in the way of acceptance and choosing to love someone. The ego is ambivalent toward others: it needs them *and* it wants to be better than them. Both of these are strategies for survival, although competing ones. So the ego has a dilemma. However, the ego isn't the only one orchestrating our life; Essence is as well. Essence is even a more important player, and it clearly prefers love over being right and superior. The ego solves its dilemma by agreeing to relationship for its own reasons and then trying to be right and superior within the relationship. Essence's intention in relationship, on the other hand, is unity, love, and joy, and that's what it brings to relationship.

What the ego brings to relationship is conditioning—lots of it. It has images and fantasies of the ideal relationship and the ideal mate. It has religious training, beliefs, and rules about sex and relationships and a man's and woman's role in them. It has information it gathered about relationships from books, movies, the Internet, soap operas, talk shows, friends, magazines, and elsewhere. It has programming that causes it to be attracted to certain qualities and features and repulsed by others.

The ego also has memories of previous relationships and of how our mother and father, and everyone else it observed, behaved in relationship. It has memories of relating to the opposite sex at every age. Some of these memories are embellished and even made up. Most of them are spun into stories by the ego, so whether they are objectively true or not, they are true to it.

The ego has opinions and preferences about everything, which are part of conditioning too. It likes and doesn't like certain foods, colors, styles, music, art, sports, movies, books, TV programs—you name it, and the ego will tell you what it likes and doesn't like about something (even if you don't want to know).

Preferences are arbitrary. They aren't based on anything—we just like something or we don't. No one's preferences are better than anyone else's. Preferences mean nothing, and they say nothing about who we really are. We are programmed to like certain things and programmed to not like certain things. Preferences are not more complicated or more important than that.

To the ego, however, preferences are very important because they give the ego an identity as someone who likes this and doesn't like that. The identities that form around the ego's preferences are who it is, and these identities are enough for the ego. But these identities aren't what make us who we are; we are much more than our preferences. However, if we believe our preferences are important, we will hold them as important and even fight over them. The ego tells us they are more important than love, but they don't even come close. Once the unimportance of preferences is seen, it's not so difficult to hold them lightly, because that's how Essence holds them.

Most relationships are based on similar conditioning—similar beliefs, similar preferences, and similar viewpoints and opinions. Similar conditioning lends itself to harmony in relationships, but there's much more to a good and satisfying relationship than this. Essence wants harmony, but not at the expense of growth. Although we might find it easier to love someone who is like us and whom we have a lot in common with, that doesn't mean a relationship with that person will be fulfilling on a spiritual level.

For a relationship to be fulfilling and not just harmonious, it also has to serve a purpose spiritually—meaning in terms of our evolution and the other person's. You and your partner are here for a reason. If you are fulfilling that purpose, you will feel fulfilled; if you aren't, you won't. *The most fulfilling relationships are ones in which the individuals are fulfilling their life purposes, either jointly or individually.* The perfect relationship for you—the one that will make you most happy on the deepest levels—is one that supports what you came into life to do. That is the best basis for relationship.

The problem is that it's often hard to assess whether or not a relationship is supporting our purpose until we are in that relationship for a while, because this kind of fulfillment needs time to unfold and be recognized. It's no wonder many relationships are unsatisfying when they are based mostly on superficial similarities and preferences rather than on something deeper. How fulfilling is it to be with someone who is like you? Fulfillment comes largely from growth, and we don't necessarily grow in relationships where harmony is the solitary goal. As important as similarities are for compatibility and harmony, they mean nothing without compatible spiritual goals or life purposes.

How do you know if someone is in your life to support what you came here to learn or accomplish? You will fall in love with that person, because that's how Essence brings people together, and the reason you fall in love may not even be related to what you find meaningful about this person later. The confusion comes from the fact that falling in love also happens between egos, so many false starts to relationship occur. Nevertheless, these attempts at relationship are often part of the process of preparing for a meaningful relationship. They serve our growth because our conditioning gets seen and smoothed out by them. Essence brings us these kinds of relationships if they are what we need for our growth.

The Ghosts That Shape Relationships

Some of the biggest players in our relationships are not even alive or real, but they have a tremendous impact nonetheless. People who shaped our conditioning, particularly our parents, are still a part of our relationships whether we realize it or not. Other people—imaginary ones—are also part of our relationships and influence them just as much as real people. People don't have to be alive or present to affect our relationships, and at least when they are, we are aware of them. The trouble with the ghosts from the past and from our imagination is that we are often not aware of their presence or their impact on our relationships.

These ghosts are fantasies, memories, and other ideas about what the partner should or shouldn't be like. It's as if they stand between us and our partner and alter our vision of him or her, for good or for bad, because they can work either way.

Here's an example of how this works: Let's say your mother had a certain shape to her body, and you found her irritating. The woman you're with has a similar shape. When you notice it, you feel turned off by it. This feeling of repulsion becomes your experience in that moment, so you conclude you must not love her and she must not be the one for you. Or it can work the other way: Your mother had a certain shape, and you loved her very much. The woman you're in love with has the same shape. When you notice it, you feel love and conclude you love her and that she's the one for you.

This feeling of attraction isn't love. Attraction is just tied to a *feeling* of love, and it is a conditioned response, not real love. The feeling of love (attraction) is just masquerading as real love. This is why we can fall in love with someone we don't even know: Falling in love is a feeling of attraction that gets triggered by something about the partner. It's a conditioned response.

Fantasies, which are a form of conditioning, are one of the most common ghosts that interfere with relating. Everyone has an image of an ideal man or woman that interferes with seeing the real person. Let's say your ideal woman is a tall, thin blonde. When you see a woman who fits this description, you imagine she has all the other qualities of your ideal woman as well—qualities that don't have anything to do with being tall, thin, and blond.

This can even happen when someone has only a slight resemblance to our ideal; the right hair or the right walk or the right way of responding might be enough for you to imagine that someone has all the qualities you desire. When this connection is made, most of the time it's so unconscious that you don't even notice the person's dissimilarities to your ideal. When you do finally see them, which is bound to happen, you feel betrayed. You feel deceived or fooled by that person when, really, you deceived yourself.

This phenomenon is obvious in dating if it happens often enough, but a similar thing happens in committed relationships. You have an image of the ideal wife or the ideal husband, and when the real person doesn't behave like that ideal, you feel angry. Although you no longer fool yourself into thinking your partner is some other way (because you know better), you still think he or she *should* behave like your ideal, or should at least try to. When your partner doesn't, you feel angry. You may judge and even attack your partner for not behaving the way you want. Instead of accepting your partner, you keep hoping he or she will change.

This tendency to expect others to meet our ideals is obviously absurd when it's pointed out, but when you're reacting to your partner falling short of your ideals, it feels absolutely reasonable. The ego assumes that its ideas—and even its fantasies—are the right ones and that it has the right to suggest that everyone else conform to them. Everyone has an equally self-centered and arrogant ego. Once you realize the arrogance of the ego, it's quite laughable, and hopefully you and your partner can learn to laugh at the immaturity and arrogance of the ego. It's immature in the sense that the ego sees the world as revolving around it, just as a child does. This point of view is about as far from the truth as you can get, which is why it causes so much suffering.

Another ghost that haunts and interferes with our relationships is the memory of people we have known. It's very common, especially in more established relationships, to react to our partner as if he or she is someone else. Instead of relating to your partner, you act as if you are relating to your mother, father, sibling, ex-partner, or someone else your partner is reminding you of in that moment. When that happens, you aren't even actually relating to that other person, but to your *idea* of that other person. Our relationships often get muddied by such memories and ideas.

Let's suppose your husband has a way of stroking your hair that reminds you of how your father touched you. Whenever your partner does that, you regress to an image of yourself as a child and behave as you did with your father. When you do this, it reminds your husband of his baby sister, whom he was very fond of. This brings out his nurturing side, which reinforces your tendency to regress. As a result, you establish a habitual father-daughter type of interaction within your relationship, which is not appropriate for lovers, but sometimes occurs in relationships.

Not only memories of people, but also memories of past incidents interfere with our relationships. We tend to react to something that is happening

---

SUMMARY: HOW FANTASIES AND MEMORIES AFFECT RELATIONSHIPS

1. Something about your partner triggers an unconscious memory of how you felt about someone else, which makes it seem like this is how you feel about your partner. You may draw conclusions about your relationship based on feelings that were triggered unconsciously by a memory.

2. When you meet someone who has even some of the qualities of your ideal woman or man, you assume he or she has all the qualities of your ideal. You don't notice the dissimilarities to your ideal.

3. You get angry at your partner when he or she doesn't live up to your image of the ideal wife or husband.

4. Your partner does something that unconsciously reminds you of someone else (e.g., your mother, father, sibling, or an ex-partner), and you react toward your partner as if he or she were that person.

5. You react to something that's happening in the present between you and your partner as you did to something similar in the past.

in the present with our partner as we did to something similar in the past. Every moment is different from every other moment, but we often respond as we did to a similar moment in the past. This is how patterns get established in relating: whenever a certain situation comes up, you react the same way. In this way, the past often shapes our present experience.

An example of this would be if your partner suggests that you straighten up the living room because guests are coming over, and you remember an argument the two of you had about keeping the house neat. So you respond defensively rather than purely to that request in that moment. Instead of letting your reaction flow out of the moment, you react to a memory—an idea.

Getting Our Needs Met in a Relationship

Most of the friction in relationships is caused by wanting our partner to be a certain way: we want our partner to talk a certain way, walk a certain way, kiss a certain way, cook a certain way, dress a certain way, drive a certain way, and take care of the house a certain way. In every respect, we have an idea about how we want our partner to be. These desires in and of themselves are not the problem. The problem is that we also feel driven to mold our partner accordingly. Why is changing our partner to suit our ideas so important to us? Why is it so hard to let the other person be the way he or she is?

We want our partner to be a certain way not for his or her sake, but for ours. Let's face it, the ego is selfish. As much as it might couch its desires in altruism, it's motivated to get certain needs met, and it expects relationship to serve those needs. Like everything else, to the ego, relationships are all about it and its needs. That's why relationships between those who are identified with the ego most of the time are doomed to difficulty. Relationships can't be about fulfilling the needs of the ego. If they are to succeed, they must be about fulfilling other deeper needs and supporting growth in the way Essence intends.

When people come together to fulfill the needs of the ego, they are never happy because what they get from the other person is never enough. Whatever the ego wants from the other person will never be enough because the ego is never satisfied with what it gets. Its *nature* is to be unsatisfied. Besides, what the ego wants and thinks will satisfy it isn't capable of providing satisfaction. What it wants are things that come and go: beauty, sex, security, status, comfort, pleasure, excitement, stimulation, fun, nurturing, and so on. Things that come and go can't provide satisfaction because they are always changing. Everything the ego treasures ebbs and flows. It's here and then it's not here. We're happy with it and then we aren't.

There's a deeper satisfaction to be had, and it isn't based on having anything but on "being." When you are happy just being, then you don't need your partner to be anything for you. You don't need anything. Then it's possible to have a truly loving relationship, one based on celebrating the truth—the ultimate reality of who you are. However, as long as you are identified with the ego, you believe you need something to be happy, and you expect your partner to provide that. Even if your partner can provide some of what you think you need, no one can provide everything because there's no end to what the ego believes it needs. When it gets something, it wants more of it or the opposite. Your partner can never win at the game of trying to provide you with what you need, and you will never be able to provide that for him or her either.

Our conditioning causes us to expect certain things from relationships. Although this conditioning varies from person to person, certain kinds of demands are typical in relationships. Because these are likely to cause problems, let's look at some of the more common demands: the expectation of sexual fulfillment, the expectation of beauty, and the expectation of being cared for.

The Expectation of Sexual Fulfillment

Sex carries some of the biggest expectations and demands. We expect our partner to meet our sexual needs and desires (our conditioning) and in so doing bring us sexual fulfillment, which we imagine to be something very wonderful. We are under the impression that orgasm is central to sexual fulfillment, and it does seem that way because the need for sex does subside afterward. However, because fulfillment doesn't come from orgasm, we often still feel unfulfilled afterward. The tendency is to attribute this lack of fulfillment to some lack in our partner, in our relationship, or in ourselves, and to fantasize that the situation might be different with someone else.

We believe that fulfillment is possible through sex. This is a deeply conditioned misunderstanding. Sex can't fulfill us any more than Twinkies can. Sex is a pleasurable experience. We give it far too much weight and importance. We think good sex will fulfill us and make us happy and make our relationship wonderful. Sex doesn't have that much power. It doesn't have the power to make us happy any more than a car or a million dollars or beauty or food or any other pleasure. It's a passing pleasure. Our conditioning around relationships makes sex seem to be the key to happiness in relationships, and it's not.

Sexual fulfillment is a lie, and one that doesn't die easily. Sex is a pleasurable experience two people share, and that's about all you can say about it. Even that's not always true—it's not always pleasurable. It has an equal potential for pain, disappointment, and suffering. We suffer over sex because it so often doesn't meet our expectations. Because we have huge expectations around it, it's bound to disappoint, and it does.

Part of developing a healthy sexual relationship is learning to let go of expectations and just be present with our partner in the moment. Happiness and fulfillment in sex comes from being present in it and present with our partner, without expectations, ideas, memories, fantasies, and other conditioning muddying and distorting the experience. Sex can be fulfilling momentarily just as any moment can be fulfilling when we are experiencing it fully.

The only fulfillment sex is capable of is the momentary fulfillment that comes by being fully present to it in the moment. The same could be said for any pleasure or anything of a passing nature: it has the potential to be fulfilling *in that moment* if we are present with it. But that passing pleasure is not going to fulfill *you* because this *you* (the ego) can never be fulfilled. It's not the ego's nature to be fulfilled; it's nature is to be dissatisfied.

The real you—Essence—is fulfilled from just being. When we are identified with Essence, then just being fulfills us, regardless of the specific experience we are having. All experience and any experience is fulfilling to Essence; it doesn't require that an experience be any particular way. When you are fully present to any experience, you feel fulfilled as well. You feel the joy of being—of experiencing. And to feel that way, it doesn't matter if sex is happening or not. It doesn't matter if anything in particular is happening.

Because of the weightiness of trying to find fulfillment in sex, meeting our sexual needs in relationship becomes more complicated than it has to be. Sex is a physical drive, and like any physical drive, it can be fulfilled even without a partner. Your partner is not in this world to fulfill your needs, including your physical needs. If there are differences in these needs, the difficulties around these differences will be much fewer if you disentangle your physical needs from your conditioning around the need for sex to be fulfilling or meaningful to your relationship.

Love is fulfilling and meaningful, but sex in and of itself is not. When love infuses the sexual experience, then sex becomes a fulfilling and meaningful experience. When this happens, it means we are aligned with Essence. However, we don't need to be experiencing sex to experience the love and fulfillment of Essence. That love and fulfillment is available in any moment.

If you are aligned with Essence while you are being sexual, the experience will be much more fulfilling than if you are aligned with the ego, because it will be loving and free of the judgments and other conditioning that interfere with joy and enjoyment. And the lighter and more enjoyable your sexual experience with your partner is, the more likely it will be repeated. In this way, being aligned with Essence is likely to improve your sex life, although that isn't the goal. Such goals are the ego's thing.

Fantasies and the Expectation of Beauty

The expectation of beauty is not an expectation only men have; women also desire an attractive partner. This particular conditioning does seem to be stronger in men than women, however. Such a demand causes a lot of unnecessary pain in relationships. We withhold love from our partner when we feel that he or she isn't fulfilling our dream of an attractive partner. We become disappointed and question our choice of partner. The partner feels this disappointment, and it's painful. The disappointment is probably something that comes and goes within the relationship depending on any number of things, but the experience of such disappointment undermines relationship and can cause both people to hold themselves at a distance from each other.

The ego dreams and fantasizes about having an attractive partner for itself. It longs for a partner who represents its particular physical ideal because it believes this will bring sexual fulfillment and happiness. When it imagines being in relationship, it's a visual experience of the partner. Other characteristics may be imagined, but for the most part, fantasies involve imaginations of how the partner will look. You imagine the partner's height, weight, eye and hair color, skin color, and facial and bodily features.

The personality characteristics we dream about are often things that make us feel good: We imagine our dream man or woman being loving and nice to us, making us laugh, and telling us how sexy and attractive we are. Our dream man or woman adores us and shows us that. Although you might actually meet someone who does feel this way about you, your day-to-day experience of him or her isn't likely to be that way. That person will be busy with other things and do all sorts of things you don't like, no matter how perfect he or she is for you.

It's helpful to notice the egocentricity and lack of realism of our fantasies because unconsciously we believe them. To the degree that we do, our partner will disappoint us. No one can live up to a fantasy—anyone's fantasy. Everyone's fantasies are somewhat the same: The beloved does and says everything you want him or her to do and say. If that weren't the case, it wouldn't be a fantasy—it would be real life. So it's good to notice that fantasies, by definition, don't match reality. They are, therefore, very poor guides for choosing a mate.

However, we are programmed to think otherwise. We really believe our fantasies indicate the kind of person we will be happiest with. We think, "If only I could find someone like that." We think that just because we dream about someone like that, we may be able to find someone like that—some-day—and then we will be so happy.

When you examine this belief, it's obvious how unreasonable it is. Have you ever met two people who are alike? Of course not. So how could you find someone like your dream man or woman? That person doesn't exist, and no amount of looking will change that. This is a deeply ingrained mis-conception and a mostly unconscious one. The more attached we are to this fantasy man or woman, the less available we will be to a real man or woman, especially one that may be quite different from this fantasy, but, neverthe-less, quite perfect for us.

We don't ever really get over our fantasies. The mind generates them whether we pay attention to them or not. So the goal isn't to get rid of them, but not to dwell on them or give them the value we usually do. We assume they give us accurate information about what we need to be happy, and that just isn't so. Life has a plan for your happiness, and it isn't given to you by way of your fantasies. It's given to you by way of real life: Life brings you the man or woman it intends for you. You don't have to go searching or spend time dreaming him or her up. When it's time for you to meet the men or women who are important to you in this lifetime, you'll be in the right place at the right time.

Essence has a way of arranging meetings by influencing you intuitively. An intuition is not a thought or fantasy, but more of a spontaneous knowing or an urge to act—to go somewhere or do something that puts you in the right place at the right time. If you don't pay attention to these intuitions, Essence tries again and keeps it up until the meeting happens. Sometimes it does take a while, but eventually most intended meetings do occur.

What a relief it is to know that it's not up to us to find the one for us, but rather that we *will* find the one for us. All we have to do is be open to recognizing him or her when this happens and be open to continuing to recognize him or her as we get to know that person and all the ways he or she doesn't meet our conditioning and expectations.

Since we all have conditioning that interferes with loving, finding reasons to not be in a relationship with someone is easy. What isn't so easy is overcoming conditioning enough to love. It comes down to this: Do you want love and relationship more than you want your desires met? Do you want love more than you want your conditioning? Even when the reward is so great, we don't necessarily choose love over conditioning. It isn't easy to overcome conditioning because, in the moment, you aren't experiencing the reward, but the conditioning, and that's often what you give your attention to and respond to.

It's sad when people who are meant to be together, and who could benefit so greatly from a union, reject it. It's a loss in so many ways because love isn't just a good feeling, but something that lends real meaning and fulfillment to life. That's what you give up when you choose conditioning over love. You get to have a *me* with all its demands and desires. You get to have it your way because you won't have to accommodate anyone else. But what you discover is that this *me* isn't happy with its demands and desires, and it isn't happy having its way, because the *me* isn't capable of being happy.

If this were really a choice between two different but equally happy ways of being, that would be one thing. But the choice is between being someone with inflexible desires and demands or just being and celebrating our divine nature with another. The ego is miserable, even when it gets its way, so having your way in partnership or having a partner that suits your ideas isn't going to make you happy anyway, even if that were a possibility.

Relationship and love call for realism over idealism. The ego encourages us not to settle for less than our ideal, while Essence presents us with the real, in every respect of the word. Only the real—what is actually present in our life rather than some possibility for love in the future—can satisfy. You will never be satisfied if you continually compare the person in front of you with someone who doesn't and will never exist. That's a recipe for unhappiness in relationship, if it even gets that far.

Physical beauty, or a lack of it, is the biggest stumbling block to love and relationship in general. Because physical appearance is so tied to fantasy, it often becomes the measure for how much we think someone will fit our other criteria for relationship. You scan the prospects for the one who looks the most appealing to you, and you go after that one. This is the ego's strategy for finding love, and it's a very poor one. For one thing, since certain characteristics are considered universally beautiful, those endowed with these attract all the interest. That leaves many people feeling like they're missing out. Even though they may pair up with others, many continue to feel this way. They imagine how wonderful it must be to be with someone who looks a certain way.

However, unless other, deeper commonalities are present, those who are with someone close to their physical ideal aren't likely to be happy either. They may experience sexual obsession, because that often accompanies attainment of the physical ideal, or they may become preoccupied with the partner maintaining his or her looks or dressing a certain way. To sustain the other's interest, the one receiving all this attention is likely to be very focused on looks as well. This is a very unhappy situation for both parties.

There's no happiness in obsession over appearances, and it takes energy and attention from other things that are more capable of providing fulfillment. In this way, physical beauty can be a curse, and those attached to having the partner look a certain way are equally cursed. It's painful to be attached and identified with something that is as ephemeral as physical beauty. The fear of losing it haunts those attached to it, and the desire to hold on to it is a burden.

The Expectation of Being Cared For

Being cared for is another expectation both men and women have, although the way each gender cares for the other is different. Men expect to be physically cared for, and women expect to be financially cared for. Our conditioning provides an unspoken agreement: "I'll do this for you if you do that for me." This conditioning was more straightforward before men's and women's roles shifted in the 1960s. After that, it became less clear what a man was expected to do for a woman and vice versa.

That's the problem with conditioning—it's not universal. If everyone had the same conditioning, life would be simpler. We would all agree on everything! But not only does everyone not have the same conditioning, but our conditioning is also always changing.

Our conditioning surrounding roles in relationships has been influenced by our culture and the times and also by our parents, who were influenced by their culture and their times. The result is quite a mixture of messages, much of it contradictory, about how men and women should be in relationship. The perfect man and perfect woman are even harder to find because our conditioning now demands that each gender be able to do everything. Rather than expecting less from our partner, which would make for more harmonious relationships, most of us expect even more. And the more stressed out we become, the more we expect from our partner. These are not easy times for relationships.

Stress is a big problem for relationships. The answer to stress tends to be to want or expect our partner to do more for us. However, these days, the partner usually feels the same way. So we find ourselves fighting over who will take care of what and how well the other person is taking care of our needs. The trouble with wanting our partner to do more for us is that it isn't our partner's responsibility to fulfill our needs, although that's a lovely side effect of a good relationship—at times. Just as often, we have our partner's needs to take care of, so that's the trade-off. When there's love, we willingly take on our partner's needs, but as soon as trouble starts, who does what for whom becomes the main battleground.

This war can never be resolved from the level of the ego because the ego never gets enough from the other person. It overlooks what the other person does and instead expects even more. It pushes for all it can get, and its lack of gratitude wears heavily on the relationship and often causes a withdrawal of love and nurturance. Who wants to be taking care of someone who demands being taken care of and doesn't appreciate what's already being done?

To get something from our partner, we will not only have to give to him or her, but also be appreciative of what we do get, which may not match what we would like. We may sometimes have to give more than what we want to give and get less than we would like. But we can't hold this imbalance against our partner, or we won't even get that much. Giving to get doesn't work because that leads to resentment if we don't get what we want. And yet not giving is the worse solution of all. Sometimes we withhold in relationships in hopes of tipping the power in our favor and, in that way, manipulating our partner to give us what we want. But withholding never works. Our partner will resent us for it and not want to give to us. From the level of the ego, there are only two options: giving to get or not giving at all. And neither of these options works. Relationships just don't work well from the level of the ego.

But how do you give to your partner when you don't feel like it? The answer is that you don't, because doing that is ultimately bad for your relationship. What you can do, however, is give to your partner what you are willing to give. Give what is natural and easiest for you to give. For example, if you don't like to cook, don't give to your partner in that way except on days when you really feel like it. Instead, ask yourself: "How do I enjoy giving?" Everyone likes doing certain things. Determine what those are and do those for your partner.

If your partner doesn't appreciate those things and demands that you do other things, it may be that he or she isn't a good match for you. You can't make yourself into the partner your partner wants. That's not the way to be in relationship. Your best chance at a happy and fulfilling relationship is to be the person you came here to be within the relationship. If that's not okay with your partner, you may not be with the right person.

If your partner is truly supportive of who you naturally are, then you will want to give to your partner. If your partner isn't supportive of who you naturally are, then you won't feel like giving to him or her. It's not surprising that many couples are unhappy with each other because what they have to offer each other is not valued by the other. Some couples aren't meant to be together, but they stay together nevertheless, for other reasons.

If you aren't feeling like giving to your partner, it's important to examine this to see what's going on, because not wanting to give to your partner may be indicative of a deeper incompatibility. In any event, this examination will reveal conditioning that needs to be understood. Often, the reason we don't feel like giving to our partner is that we are angry with him or her for not complying with our desires or other conditioning.

Anger over unmet desires (conditioning) causes us to withdraw our love and shut down our heart. The ego tries to manipulate others with anger and withdrawal to try to get them to do what it wants, but that tactic always backfires. Who wants to cooperate with an angry, unloving ego? And if they do cooperate, they are bound to feel resentful. All anger accomplishes is bringing the partner to the same level of consciousness, one that is contracted and unloving, and that just doesn't feel good. When we feel angry, it's an opportunity to discover something about our conditioning—not a sign that our partner needs to change.

When our needs and expectations aren't met in relationship, the ego reacts with anger and possibly threats, blame, name-calling, and other measures designed to manipulate the partner. This is also how children act. Children are egocentric and expect the world to fulfill their needs. That's exactly how the ego is, which is why it's no more capable of having a healthy romantic relationship than a child is.

If a relationship is to be a happy one, it can't be about need fulfillment. It has to be about much more than that. We need to expect more from our relationships than just need fulfillment. We need to expect love and a deeper connection, and that will never happen from the level of the ego. To the ego, relationships are all about need fulfillment; to Essence, they are about love.

We make the mistake of thinking that fulfilling each other's needs is the purpose of relationship and even the way to express love. Although it's true that when we love someone, we often gladly give to them, it's not true that love or relationship is about fulfilling the needs of another. That happens, but that's not the purpose of relationship. It may be the purpose of relationships between egos, but it's not the purpose of an Essence-based relationship, whose purpose is love.

Love is not about needs, but about seeing beyond our conditioned needs and desires to the Essence of the other person and sharing at that level. Essence's purpose in relationships is to experience Oneness with another—to

SUMMARY: GIVING AND GETTING

1. Your partner is not in this world to take care of your needs, and you are not in this world to take care of your partner's needs. Don't expect your partner to take care of you. Anything he or she does is a gift. Expect more from your relationship than need fulfillment. Expect love.

2. Acknowledge what your partner does give and be sure to express gratitude for that, even if it's not what you specifically asked for or desired. Gratitude will keep the love flowing.

3. To get, you will have to give, but giving to get doesn't work. What you give to your partner must come from a sincere desire to give.

4. Don't give in a way that you aren't willing to give. That will only lead to resentment. Give only in a way that you are willing to give.

5. Give in ways that are the most natural to you. Determine the ways you most enjoy giving, and give in those ways.

6. Don't withhold from your partner in an attempt to manipulate him or her.

7. Examine why you don't feel like giving to your partner. Uncover the conditioning behind any anger. It's just conditioning and not worth losing love over.

8. Be the person you came here to be. Don't try to be the partner your partner wants you to be.

9. Look beyond your conditioned needs and desires to the Essence of your partner.

10. Be grateful for the opportunity to celebrate life with someone.

experience love. It has no other purpose. It's not trying to get anything from the other. It's just happy to be with the other and celebrate that beingness together.

Here is a summary of how to approach giving and getting in a way that will get you what you *really* want: love.

The Biggest Illusion of All

Illusions cause pain in relationships because they distance us from the real person in front of us and from the very real experience of the present moment. Illusions, or false ideas or fantasies, cause us to disengage from what is true and real right now. They cause us to believe in something that isn't showing up in this moment and isn't likely to ever show up. Whenever we disengage from real life—from the aliveness of the present moment and whatever is showing up in that moment—we suffer. Being divorced from Essence is painful, and our illusions do that.

The biggest illusion that harms and undermines relationships is that romance and sexual passion can and should last. The truth is that they don't. It's wonderful when romance and passion are showing up, but those moments pass, and the relationship matures (hopefully) into something else. Romance and passion are replaced by love when all goes well. Romance and passion belong to the beginning of a relationship. Have you ever known it to be otherwise? That's not to say there isn't any romance or passion in long-term relationships, but the intense feelings of breathlessness, excitement, elation, butterflies, and longing in the beginning of a relationship don't last.

Romance and passion don't have much to do with love. *They are what bring people together to explore and grow in love.* If you don't understand this, you will be very disappointed when they disappear, and in fact, this is why many people do go from relationship to relationship. They believe that romance and passion are identical to love and that if these things aren't there, the relationship must not be right. The disappearance of romance and passion often coincide with projections dropping away and differences and challenges showing up. Some people deal with this by looking elsewhere. Those who are fortunate (or unfortunate) enough to be attractive often find plenty of other opportunities.

Relationships and love require a willingness to commit to someone and adjust to differences, while the search for romance and passion doesn't. Some people jump from one relationship to another, enjoying those wonderful feelings as long as they last. Romance and passion can be like a drug for some, and like an addict, they may never get beyond these things to something more fulfilling.

This truth, that romance and passion are a passing phase in relationships, may come as a disappointment; however, what follows romance and passion is much more fulfilling because it promises both growth and love. Romance and passion aren't sustainable because they would interfere with life; you would never get out of bed! So although romantic, passionate times are wonderful, and we love to relive them through movies and books, romance and passion aren't what sustain us. Just as dessert is delightful, but doesn't support our overall well-being, romance and passion too are delightful, but not substantial enough to fulfill our deepest need as human beings to love.

The tragedy of misunderstanding the role of romance and passion in relationships is not only that many go from relationship to relationship looking for "the one" who will fulfill them romantically, but also that so many who are in a relationship that's right for them dream of someone else who will always make them feel a certain way. This dream is an illusion that can keep us from really committing and being present to the beloved in front of us, the one that life has brought to us, for better or worse.

Rather than looking for someone who will make us feel butterflies and goose bumps, being present to the one we are with from Essence will allow us to feel the love and connection we have always wanted. This love is more real, more fulfilling, and more substantial than butterflies and goose bumps. It often isn't for lack of the right partner that we don't feel this real love, but for lack of alignment with our own Essence and the Essence of another.

5

MOVING BEYOND CONDITIONING

What Drives Conditioning

Regardless of what the conditioning is, because it is conditioning, it's a problem in relationships. Differences in conditioning are the cause of most disagreements in relationships. This problem would seem simple enough to solve: don't give in to your conditioning; don't be attached to having things the way you want them. Although simple, it's not easy to do; if it were easy, we wouldn't have so much trouble getting along with others. What makes it so difficult to ignore our conditioning? Let's take a moment to examine this question.

Spending time examining conditioning this way helps diffuse its power, so it has less ability to determine our behavior. Seeing that there's nothing behind our feelings but ideas and images puts our feelings in perspective. They no longer feel so true either. We tend to believe that our feelings tell us something true and meaningful about a situation and that they deserve some action. But most feelings come from conditioning that has little truth or relevance now, in this moment. Our conditioning is just a set of ideas we were given, much of it a long time ago. Giving our conditioning power by letting it guide our actions and reactions only leads to unhappiness and discord in our relationships. What if you just let it be there without doing anything about it?

EXERCISE: EXAMINING WHAT DRIVES CONDITIONING

Think of a time when conditioning came up, perhaps sometime when you didn't feel loving toward your partner because of something he or she did or some way he or she looked. What desires, demands, or expectations were behind that feeling? Did an image arise in your mind (possibly unconsciously) that related to or fed that feeling?

Make a list all of the things you said to yourself, subtly or not so subtly, and all the images that arose around this feeling. Examine each one and ask yourself, "Is that true?" It might be helpful to investigate where this conditioning or image came from. Does it relate to your father, mother, a sibling, a former partner, or someone else in your past? Perhaps it's simply cultural conditioning.

Our conditioning would be easier to ignore if it weren't so tied to our identity—to a sense of who we are and who we should be. For instance, for some men, driving a car that is clean and shiny is important to their identity—to how they feel about themselves. So if their car gets dirty, it's upsetting to them. When someone's reactions are out of proportion to an event, you can be sure that identity is involved. To investigate conditioning like this, try asking, "What if I didn't do or have that?" For example, "What if I didn't have a clean and shiny car?" The answers you come up with reveal the meaning you give to doing or having something, in this case, having a clean and shiny car: "If my car isn't clean and shiny, that means I'm lazy, I'm irresponsible, I don't look good, I don't have money, others won't respect me, and so on."

We give much more meaning to things than they deserve, and that's why some conditioning is hard to ignore. If we don't follow it, we feel bad about ourselves. We feel our value as a person is diminished—and that's never the case, except in the ego's eyes. You can take the ego's point of view, if you like, but doing so only leads to suffering and conflict with others.

So some conditioning is difficult to ignore because we feel our identity and value hinge on following it. You see yourself as someone who does things this way and not that way, who feels this way and not that way, who believes this and not that, who likes this and doesn't like that, who wants this and doesn't want that, who knows about this and doesn't know about that. When you think of yourself, you think of your ideas, your beliefs, your opinions, your likes and dislikes, your desires, your fantasies, and your dreams. All of these are part of your conditioning, which gives you a sense of being someone. If your partner disagrees with your conditioning or interferes with carrying it out, you feel personally threatened.

We mistake our conditioning for who we are, so naturally we fight over it because it feels like we are fighting for our life. Giving up our conditioning feels like we are giving up our identity. We are afraid if we give up these ideas, we won't be who we are. Then who would we be? The ego feels confused and frightened about this possibility. It feels like it won't exist, and that's true: without ideas, the ego doesn't exist. But *you* still do.

Ideas give us an identity, but they aren't responsible for our existence. We just don't realize that we don't need an identity to exist, so we cling to our ideas, as if they were necessary for our existence. When we are aligned with Essence, we realize how joyful it is to exist without our ideas.

Another reason it's difficult to ignore our conditioning is that we believe it. When we think something, we believe it's right because it is our thought. We think our conditioning is the right conditioning and that others should be like us. Even if we aren't under the illusion that they should be like us, we still wish they would be, and we try to win them over to our way of seeing or doing things. Wishing they were like us is a slightly gentler and more enlightened position than assuming others should be like us, but the result is still conflict and a lack of acceptance of the other person's point of view.

Ignoring and Accommodating Our Partner's Conditioning

There are two ways to keep out of trouble in our relationships. The first is to ignore our own conditioning—our desires and ideas about how things should be. The second is to ignore or accommodate our partner's conditioning. Trouble starts when we are attached to having our own conditioning met, when we try to change our partner's conditioning, or when we let our

EXERCISE: NOTICING THE ENERGY BEHIND THE "I"

When you express your conditioning by saying "I like," "I want," "I think," or something similar, notice the energy behind these phrases. Notice the excitement and attachment around expressing what you think and what you like. This is the energy of the ego, and it drives much of our verbal expression. Notice how often what you say has this energy behind it, and know that when you feel this energy, the ego is speaking.

Start to notice the difference between the ego speaking and speech that comes from Essence. When you speak from Essence, it's free of this energy, this push to express yourself and get your point across. Essence has no need to get its point across. It doesn't have an agenda like the ego has. Notice this difference and choose not to speak "I want" and "I like" as many times as the ego is used to speaking them. By indulging in this habit less often it will lose its strength and become less unconsciously driven. Practice just being and allowing whatever is happening to happen without expressing an opinion or judgment about it. That is Essence's way.

partner's conditioning trigger our own. So much of the conditioning that causes difficulties in relationships is very minor and wouldn't be a problem if we would let our partner do things the way he or she does them, without trying to change it just because it's different from how we do things. Does it really matter if your partner doesn't wring out the dishrag after using it? Or leaves hair or toothpaste in the sink? Or has bad table manners? Or drives too cautiously? Or insists on reading the newspaper in the morning before doing anything else? These and so many other little things that annoy us in relationship are just not important. They are not more important than love. Can you just let them go? Can you just let your partner be the way he or she is?

If you can, the rewards are great. He or she will surely love you. Acceptance allows your partner to relax and just be. It allows him or her to drop into Essence, and from Essence love flows. This acceptance will come back to you, so you can just relax and be in Essence too. Acceptance is quite simple, really, but it's powerful. It's wise not to underestimate its importance in relationships. Acceptance is a quality of Essence, and when you choose it, you choose Essence over the ego.

In many cases, accepting our partner's way of being is just a matter of counteracting any complaints the ego has with a positive statement of acceptance, such as, "Let it be," "Everything is perfect," "Love is more important than this," or "He's just the way he is." These are expressions of truth from Essence, and we can use expressions like these to neutralize or change our relationship to our egoic mind, which judges and resists the many ways our partner is different from us. We can remind ourselves: "That's just the ego. There it goes again, trying to cause trouble!" Conflict is not inevitable in relationships, and we can learn to avoid it through ignoring our partner's conditioning and letting him or her just be the way he or she is. This is one of the greatest gifts we can give our partner.

As part of this acceptance, we can even go along with our partner's conditioning (desires) sometimes, out of kindness. For instance, if your partner wants you to drive a little faster, why not? Or if she wants you to wring out the dishrag or keep the bathroom sink clean, why not? Why wouldn't we do these little things if they please our partner? People who love and accept and respect each other sometimes do what doesn't come naturally; they do so out of love, to maintain harmony, which is good for everyone. We do these little things because they are good for the relationship. We put the relationship and love before our own tendencies. Doing things the way we do them is not more important than love. When we live with someone, being flexible and considerate in small ways yields a big result: love. The ego is not cooperative and considerate; only Essence is. When we emulate Essence, we always win.

With all this talk about accepting conditioning, it is important to be clear that not all conditioned behavior *should* be accepted. Behavior that is abusive is not acceptable, not only because no one deserves abuse, but also because a relationship can't survive it. You don't accept abusive actions and speech from your partner because you value yourself, because abusive actions and speech are not good for your relationship, and because it's not good for your partner to be allowed to behave that way. Essence accepts, but it doesn't accept abuse because it is pro-life and pro-love. Essence doesn't allow itself to be victimized. It says no to negativity, hatred, and abuse. To do anything else is to be an accomplice to or enabler of negativity and harm.

Putting your foot down in this regard is a simple matter of stating that you won't tolerate your partner speaking to you or behaving toward you in an abusive way. Anything you or your partner have to say to each other can be stated clearly, cleanly, and without blame, anger, judgment, or criticism. It is imperative that you learn to speak to each other this way rather than in a way that creates further negativity. There are lots of books available that teach how to communicate nonviolently. It's unfortunate that this most important skill isn't taught in school.

We are here to learn love, and relationships teach this. If your relationship isn't helping you to learn love, but, instead, is fostering enmity, then you need to consider leaving it. If interactions within your relationship are overwhelmingly negative or abusive, and you are unable to turn that behavior around, then it's likely that you and your partner aren't meant to be together. If you have tried everything you can to transform the negativity within you and within your relationship and you haven't succeeded, then staying in the relationship might not be appropriate. Sometimes love means loving yourself enough to leave a negative or an abusive situation.

How to Avoid Being Triggered by Your Partner's Conditioning

When our partner is judging us or confronting us with something he or she doesn't like about us or about what we are doing, the natural response is a defensive one, which is how most arguments begin. We explain our point of view or argue our position. Just as you can learn to recognize the ego within yourself when it's operating and say no to it and stay in Essence, you can learn to see the ego operating in others and say no to the temptation to jump into ego identification and join it in a fight with your partner.

When you are in Essence, your response to your partner's ego identification and contraction is compassion. You know what it feels like to be ego identified, contracted, angry, and judgmental. It doesn't feel good. Your partner is suffering, even though he or she may be trying to blame or hurt you. Essence feels compassion when it sees this happening in another. It doesn't take the partner's words and actions personally. It realizes that the partner is caught up in a state of consciousness that is irrational—a state of unconsciousness. It also realizes that this state will pass and that the best thing to do when he or she is in this state is to give the partner attention and love.

If you are able to acknowledge your partner's pain and point of view, this will help him or her to relax and soften. Arguing with your partner or defending your point of view only keeps your partner attached to the ego's position. "I can see this is really important to you." "I'll try to remember next time to do this." "You're right." "I could have been more considerate." "I'm sorry." These are the kinds of words that can defuse the tension between you.

One of the worst things you can do when your partner is angry with you is to point out that he or she is caught in the ego. Making your partner wrong will only bring out more defensiveness, anger, and criticism. Instead, try saying things that will make it easier for your partner to drop into the Heart, or Essence. You can help your partner drop into the Heart by acknowledging where he or she is coming from: "You work really hard, and I should have been more helpful." "I should have realized this was important to you." "I should have been more considerate of your feelings." "I should have thought of doing that." Saying such things is plain and simple kindness and compassion that naturally flows from Essence. It is not being weak. It's choosing love and choosing your relationship over any need you might have to be right.

The Power of "I'm Sorry"

When we find ourselves in conflict because we are insisting that our partner do something our way or because we are reacting to the way our partner happens to be doing something, there's a simple way out: apologize. Notice the negative effect that what you are saying or doing is having on the relationship, stop doing it, and apologize. It's never too late to say "I'm sorry." These are tremendously healing words. They can stop a conflict instantly and drop both people into their Hearts because "I'm sorry" comes from Essence. "I'm sorry" concedes that you were wrong in pushing for what you were pushing for. It stops the ego, which is trying to be right, in its tracks, and immediately allows the partner to relax and feel sympathy and love for you.

When we are able to acknowledge that the ego is running us, it loses its power over us. It's only when we act it out unconsciously that it has power, but as soon as Essence comes in enough for us to be conscious of what's happening, the ego's game can't continue. The jig is up, the ego's been seen, and it can no longer run us. This turning point requires a willingness to admit you were wrong, and that's the hardest part. But once you see that what's been driving you to hurt or manipulate your partner is the ego trying to be right, then it becomes much easier to let go, be humbled, and say "I'm sorry." You don't have to defend the ego's position because you see that the ego isn't who you are anyway. It's just that part in all of us that causes suffering to ourselves and others.

It's surprising how just saying "I'm sorry" softens you and your partner. Suddenly, there's nothing more to argue over because you have conceded the fight. There's no more reason to withhold your love, which we often do to try to manipulate our partner, and the result is that love begins to flow again. Suddenly, you both remember what you love about each other. It's funny how the ego clouds this, but it does so only momentarily if we are willing to concede our position and apologize for any hurt we may have caused. Your partner will love you for that, and more important perhaps, apologizing makes it possible for you to love your partner again.

The Importance of Forgiveness

When we forgive our partner for being ego identified and for everything that comes with that (e.g., anger, unkindness, manipulation, judgment, and blame), that allows us to stay in Essence, which is its own reward and why forgiveness is actually not so hard to do. It feels good to forgive because goodness and Essence feel good. Isn't it interesting how life rewards us for goodness, while following the ego feels really bad? Life has a built-in self-correcting mechanism!

Without forgiveness, we jump into ego identification and try to prove our partner wrong and ourselves right. Forgiveness, on the other hand, allows us to accept that our partner is in ego identification and to love him or her anyway, and this is what allows our partner to drop into Essence and out of the ego. Forgiveness allows us to stay in Essence, and it brings our partner into Essence.

Forgiving ourselves is just as important, for the same reason. To forgive yourself for being ego identified and all that comes with it requires seeing that you are ego identified, and this breaks the spell of ego identification. As soon as you see you are ego identified, you are outside of it and you have some choice—to either reidentify with the ego or not. At this point, you can decide to stop trying to defend your position. Instead, you see that your position was, in fact, the ego's position and not yours at all! You forgive yourself for being human, and that forgiveness allows you to experience Essence.

However, as long as you are identified with your ego's position, you won't see that there's anything to forgive. To forgive yourself, you first have to see that your position isn't necessarily the best or only position, and the ego doesn't want to concede this. If your partner is in Essence and not in the ego, this will be easier for you to see.

What you can notice when you are identified with the ego is how bad this makes you feel, not to mention how bad it makes your partner feel. And you can acknowledge that feeling bad isn't what you want. You want to feel good. You want to feel love. So you forgive yourself for being human because you don't want to suffer anymore. You see that you can have your position and suffer, or you can feel good and be loving. All it takes to free yourself from suffering is to forgive yourself for being human—for having an ego. It isn't your fault anyway.

Forgiveness also allows us to let go of the past, which is the source of a lot of trouble in relationships. We forgive the past because the only alternative is to bring the suffering of the past into this precious moment, and doing that simply doesn't make any sense. It makes sense to the ego because it would rather have its position and suffer than be wrong, but the ego is the irrational part of us. Essence's wisdom and point of view are available in any moment if we allow ourselves to drop out of our mind and into the moment, where it can be accessed.

Essence is accessed through our intuition, not through our mind. When we drop into our body and senses and out of our mind, we experience life and our partner as Essence does. From Essence, forgiveness is easy because Essence feels only love, compassion, and acceptance. It sees the truth in your partner, and it sees the falseness of your own ego. From Essence, it's possible to let go of past and current positions and all the pain they entail.

They don't do you any good anyway. You don't need any of them to be who you really are! You don't need your ego! What a relief and what freedom to discover that suffering is unnecessary and just a matter of choosing to put your attention on something other than your ideas of what you want, what you like, what you think, what you wish, and what was.

And Forget

We all do stupid, careless, or hurtful things that we later regret. If relationships are to last, we have to find a way to not only forgive these indiscretions, but also forget them. Forgiveness alone isn't quite enough if we bring memories of these wrongs into the present moment, which is sure to revitalize them and the feelings around them. We need to leave them in the past, where they belong.

Fortunately, there is only one way the past hurts can be brought into the present, and that is through thought, which is something we have some control over. Although we may not have control over a thought arising, we do have the power either to feed it by giving our attention to it or to turn away from it. Even though turning away isn't always easy, it's infinitely easier than the alternative, which only produces suffering for everyone.

One of the reasons the memory of a transgression isn't ignored is because the one who was wronged often wants to punish the other by bringing up the transgression, rejecting the other, or being hurtful in return. That's the ego's way of dealing with having been hurt. But inflicting pain on others is no solution to having been hurt. Doing this only creates more pain, not only for others, but also for us. It feels terrible to be hateful and unkind. Those who hurt us deserve our compassion, not revenge, because they must be suffering a lot to have done so. It feels bad to be identified with the ego and its hatred, anger, and negativity. Why join those who are being hurtful by adding more hurt to the situation?

When we are the one who caused the harm or hurt, we sometimes dwell on the memory of it as a way of punishing ourselves or to try to atone for what we did. But this too is an ineffective strategy on the part of the ego and only keeps us identified with the ego and the pain. Guilt is a way the ego keeps us identified with it. Forgiving ourselves and not bringing the memory of the incident into the present is the only thing that can free us from the ego and the pain it causes. Forgetting the incident doesn't mean you won't learn from it—you undoubtedly will. It just means you won't continue to suffer over it. Suffering doesn't serve anyone or anything. It's unnecessary and a sign that we are identified with the ego. When you see the truth of this, ignoring such memories becomes easier. They don't serve you, your partner, or your relationship. Bringing these memories into the present moment only serves the ego, which is always trying to be right, even long after an event has passed. That's really what these memories are about. Bringing them into the present is the ego's highly ineffective way of trying to fix, defend, or exact retribution for something that happened in the past—and none of these things is possible.

Bringing thoughts about the past into the present fortifies the pain of an event and makes it more likely that that memory will come up more regularly. It causes you to reexperience the pain, and it reinforces the tendency to dwell on such thoughts and keep the pain going. The mind will chew on such things like a dog on a bone, refusing to let go. But unlike a bone, these memories can never be fully chewed and digested by thinking about them; that merely ensures the perpetuation of pain.

The only way the pain from the past can be stopped is through a conscious act of will to not dwell on painful memories when they arise. Dwelling on them only creates a painful present. We are free to choose, of course, and many do choose to dwell on those memories for a very long time. But it's exhausting, and it destroys relationships. Do you want love more than this pain and drama? The ego actually doesn't, but Essence does. When you are able to find that place within you that is willing to forgive *and* forget, then love is possible.

Something more than forgiving and forgetting is required when relationships are abusive, however. By all means, forgive those who have abused you and forgive yourself for having allowed it and forget it—but also leave the situation. In these cases, you forgive the abuser and yourself and forget the abuse for your own well-being so that you won't be burdened by anger, blame, hatred, shame, self-blame, guilt, sadness, regret, and resentment. Forgiving, forgetting, and leaving are the gifts you give to yourself, because you don't deserve abuse or the painful feelings that come from it.

Using Humor to Break Ego Identification

When it comes from Essence, humor can be very healing. It can move us out of identification with the ego, which takes its desires and ideas (conditioning) too seriously. The ego gets upset about even relatively small things. When we are identified with it, we lose our perspective, our ability to see the larger picture, and often we get angry and even blame our partner. Small things seem huge and overly important: a broken dish, forgetting to get something at the store, being late for dinner, a stain on a favorite shirt, having to wait in line, losing a paper. This magnification and shortsightedness cause so much pain in relationships, and it doesn't have to be that way. A little humor can go a long way in bringing the perspective of Essence back.

If our partner is identified with the ego, there are ways we can bring humor to the situation—without making fun of him or her, of course. Humor can bring people back into the Heart. Here are some examples:

"You're always getting stains on your shirt!"

"I resemble that remark!"

"I don't know what to do with you. You're always forgetting or losing something."

"I don't know what to do with me either."

"I hate that when you use that expression; it reminds me of my father."

"Just so it doesn't remind you of your mother!"

"It drives me crazy when you lose your keys!"

"I have that effect on people sometimes."

Some of these replies are funny because the responder is agreeing that his or her humanness is a problem. The agreeableness of the response disarms the ego and has a way of winning over the other's heart. And of course, it helps if you deliver that line with a big smile. In general, agreeing with our partner is a simple way to disarm the ego and bring peace to the situation.

Using humor this way can be a little tricky, though. The way you know you've pulled it off is if both you and your partner smile or laugh and the tension lifts. If your humor truly comes from Essence, it will bring the other person into Essence.

If you can't come up with a funny reply, you can try disarming the ego with sweetness:

"Stop tracking mud into the house!"

"Only if you promise to let me give you a back rub later."

"You're always late."

"I missed you every minute."

"Why did you forget that?"

"I must have lost my head over you."

Expressing Gratitude

Gratitude is a quality of Essence, and when we are feeling it, we are in Essence. When we are not feeling it, expressing it anyway can get us to feel it, and expressing gratitude will also help our partner drop into Essence. Expressing gratitude is good for you and good for your partner. It's a simple thing you can do that will help you and your partner live more from Essence.

It's surprising how uplifting gratitude, even over little things, can be: "I love that you remembered to do that." "You're so wonderful at fixing things." "I appreciate how sweet you are." Giving and receiving gratitude for something small feels just as good as giving and receiving it for something big. The small things that our partner does for us are so often overlooked and taken for granted, but they are real opportunities to express our gratitude and thus keep the good feelings going in our relationship.

There's always something to be grateful for—just the fact that you and your partner are together for another day (someday this will no longer be true), that you can function as you do, that you have what you have. The fact that someone is willing to do anything for us is quite a miracle; it's an act of love. These acts of love are natural to Essence, but not natural at all to the ego. Every act of giving without trying to get something in return comes from Essence.

Tension in relationships is often caused by not feeling appreciated, and gratitude is the antidote to that. A lack of appreciation for our partner and what he or she does comes from being identified with the ego. When we are identified with the ego, we notice what someone *hasn't* done for us. And we don't notice what he or she *has* done for us, so we don't feel appreciation. We take for granted the good qualities and good acts of our partner and, instead, focus on what else we want. We demand more, without appreciating what we have. We forget what we fell in love with about our partner, and we want more or something different. We forget to express gratitude because we don't feel appreciative. But this lack of appreciation can be turned around by simply expressing gratitude, whether you feel it or not.

When you are identified with the ego, your partner is bound to feel unappreciated. And when your partner feels unappreciated, he or she wants to be acknowledged by you. When you do that, his or her ego can relax because, even though the ego doesn't express appreciation, it does expect to receive it! When your partner experiences appreciation, your partner's ego is soothed, and he or she can drop into Essence. Often, it isn't that your partner isn't willing to give to you; it's that your partner just wants to be acknowledged and appreciated for giving.

A little appreciation goes a long way in relationships. It results in cooperation, in the willingness to be helpful to each other, while a lack of appreciation results in the withdrawal of love and giving, which can have a very negative, spiraling effect. To turn this negative spiral around, gratitude, appreciation, praise, and compliments do wonders. Sometimes that's all that is needed for harmony, happiness, and love to flow once again.

"Always" and "Never" Are Never True

When you hear the words "always" and "never" coming out of your mouth or your partner's, you can be sure that the ego is engaged. The ego tells stories, and it loves to tell stories about how the partner "always" or "never" does something. Notice how right and self-righteous you feel when you use these words. The ego uses them because doing so lends authority to what it's saying. It uses these words to convince you of its case.

However, this strategy generally backfires because the result is usually a fight. These are fighting words. They draw out the other person's ego, which tries to defend its position. It argues, "That isn't true! I don't always do that." It's just as likely to add, "Well, you never . . ." These fights can't be won by anyone because both positions are false: No one always or never does the kinds of things he or she is being accused of. And yet such dialogues are seriously engaged in by egos.

These are two words to watch out for and eliminate from your vocabulary in describing someone else's behavior. It's very offensive to hear from your partner that you always or never do something when you undoubtedly can come up with many examples to the contrary. It's offensive because it doesn't acknowledge all the times you did do what your partner wanted you to do. It's offensive not only because it's untrue, but also because it's so unappreciative. When we are on the receiving end of this language, it makes us angry. It makes us want to fight or withdraw, and neither is what anyone really wants.

What do we really want when we use these words? Usually, we are trying to get our partner to do something or to stop doing something: "You always leave your dishes in the sink" is intended to change that behavior. So why not just ask for that? Using "always" or "never" instead of just asking makes the other person wrong, and the ego loves to make the other person wrong because it loves to be right.

But this is a terrible strategy for relationships! Making your beloved wrong is not going to enhance love and cooperation; it will only break down your relationship. If you are serious about having love in your life, you have to see through the ego's damaging ways and not allow them to undermine your relationship. Why are relationships so difficult? Because egos make them so. The ego's desire to be right and make the partner wrong is some of our most destructive programming.

The good news is that "always" and "never" are very clear tip-offs that the ego is at work. So don't give in to speaking this way to your partner, and it will be much easier for your partner to not give in to it either. You can even make a pact—a pact between Essence and Essence—to avoid using these words with each other.

Essence's Touches

Have you noticed how soothing a touch can be? Even from a stranger, a touch, when it is from Essence, calms and softens us. Of course, the ego touches too, and that's very different. You can tell the difference quite easily because each kind of touch feels different. The ego touches to get something, while Essence touches to give something. When Essence touches, it's a reaching out, acknowledging unity with someone.

As a result, touch can be powerful in breaking down walls and softening hearts in relationships. If someone is angry at you, and you put your hand on him or her or move close, that person is likely to relax. This touch is a way of communicating agreement, sympathy, empathy, and unity, which is quite the opposite of what the ego in that situation communicates. When you feel like replying in anger, stopping, getting close to the other person, and touching him or her caringly can defuse not only that person's anger, but also any tendency you might have to reply from your ego.

When couples sit or lie down close together as they are communicating something difficult, that communication is much more likely to come from Essence rather than from the ego. Being physically close to your partner while communicating is a very simple thing you can do to avoid or smooth conflicts in your relationship. From Essence, anything that needs to be communicated can be communicated in a way that is loving rather than blaming, hurtful, or judgmental. Or you may decide to communicate nothing at all. The important thing is to wait to communicate difficult things until you are in Essence and can communicate from there. Touch will help you and your partner move into Essence and stay there while you are doing that.

A Spiritual Practice to Improve Relationships

If you look closely, you will see how thinking and talking about others is usually only in service to the ego and its need to be superior and right. Thinking and talking about others rarely serves any other purpose. Sometimes we do need to talk about others to convey information, but too often our thoughts and speech turn into a position, an opinion, a judgment, or a story about them. The ego is always taking a position; that's its job—to form an opinion and take a stance on everything, and both are part of its strategy to make itself superior. From there, the ego builds a story (e.g., "She does that just to make me mad"), and this story becomes the lens through which we see the other person.

The ego takes a stance (e.g., "I'm smarter than he is") often by first forming a judgment (e.g., "He's not very bright when it comes to finances"), and it assumes that its stance is the correct one. This is the way the ego gets to feel superior. Thoughts like these are an attempt to manage our self-image. Often others don't even know this is going on, but these opinions, positions, conclusions, and judgments interfere with relating to others purely, simply, and spontaneously in the moment. We bring our judgments, stories, and position into the moment, and they color the interaction and thereby change it. Although others may not consciously be aware of our judgments, stories, or position, unconsciously they often are.

If all these thoughts about others did not go on, then what comes out of our mouths when we were with them would much more likely come from Essence than the ego. When we spend time thinking about others, it's difficult for these thoughts to not affect our interactions and communications with them. If these thoughts were never indulged in, they simply wouldn't be a problem. Imagine what it would be like to interact with others without judgments and preconceptions, just based on what arises within you to say and do in the moment. That is living in Essence.

Another benefit of living without thoughts about others is that it frees us from the tendency to be concerned about what others think of us. When we aren't thinking about others in a judgmental way, we also lose concern for any judgments others may have for us. Judgments are seen as false within us and in others. We are removed from the whole judgment game.

The way to living without judgments is simply to see the truth about them: they don't serve us or others. The ego leads us to believe they are important, relevant, and useful, and they just aren't. Once we see this, we are free to not indulge in them. They may arise in the mind out of habit, but eventually, if we don't give them our attention, this habit of thinking and talking about others will subside.

This is an important spiritual practice. We all know that gossip isn't a good thing, but the ego loves to gossip and finds excuses and rationalizations for doing it anyway. This egoic pleasure isn't worth the destructiveness it causes to relationships—and to our own sense of self. The truth is that it doesn't feel good to be involved in the ego's agenda. We don't feel good about ourselves when we do this. When the full ramifications of thinking and speaking about others are taken into account, it just isn't worth it.

The more clearly these ramifications are seen, the more easily the habit of thinking and talking about others can be broken. What you discover once you give up thinking and talking about others is that it's such a relief to not take a position or tell a story. Once you realize how much energy the ego expends on uselessly thinking and talking about others, and how that activity puts you in a place of contraction that just doesn't feel good, you'll choose not to do it.

6

MOVING BEYOND DIFFERENCES

Differences Don't Have to Be a Problem

Although differences often result in conflict and disharmony in relationships, they don't have to. You already accept lots of differences
about your partner, and many of them you even like. Differences can be
interesting and stimulating, depending on how you look at them. Actually,
any difference could be seen as interesting instead of wrong or problematic.
It's just that the ego defines certain differences as bad because of conditioning. Even this conditioning doesn't have to be a problem if you don't pay
attention to what your egoic mind is saying.

So what if the mind doesn't like something? You are not the mind, and
when you realize that, what it says isn't a problem. It's only when we are
identified with the mind ("I think it, therefore it's true") that differences
become a problem, because then we believe what comes next: the mind's as-
sertion of what needs to be done about that problem. We believe the mind's
solution to the "problem" of differences, which usually involves trying to
change something about our partner.

For example, your mind says of your partner, "I wish he would sit up
straight. He looks so slouchy the way he sits—and so short. I like tall men."
This thought isn't really a problem. The mind chatters on and has opinions
all the time. This thought is only a problem if you agree with it! If you do,
you have a problem—what to do about his slouching. Next, the egoic mind

gladly jumps in with reasons for changing his posture: "Slouching isn't good for his health. Slouching is unattractive. He'll be stooped over when he gets older." It pulls out every fact and belief it's got about posture, but the truth is, the ego just wants him to be different than he is. It's not really concerned about his health and well-being, and certainly not his happiness. It just wants him to fit its conditioning—what it likes and finds attractive. If you believe the case the mind has made against slouching, you will take this case to him and try to convince him. Unfortunately, nagging people is a very poor strategy for changing them, and it only alienates them. It's not that there isn't some truth to conditioning; that's one of the reasons it's difficult to ignore. It's just that imposing our conditioning on others hurts our relationships.

The egoic mind has lots of ideas about what it likes and how things should be done, and it offers them nearly constantly: "You should sit up straight and not slouch," for example. When we are identified with it, we agree with it. Like a soldier, we obey our orders without even questioning them. We don't examine the reason for doing something a certain way. We just think, "This is how you're supposed to do things."

We heard a lot about how things should be done when we were growing up. Children are taught how to make a bed, how to brush their teeth, how to dress themselves—how to do everything. For many things, this teaching was useful. Being shown how to do certain things saved us a lot of trouble. We benefited from this kind of information being passed on, although even with these things, there wasn't just one way to do them. This kind of conditioning really isn't a problem except when we try to impose it on others, as so often happens in relationships.

If how to make a bed or how to brush your teeth were the only kinds of things couples disagreed on, then disagreements might be more easily resolved. However, the ego has lots of other ideas about how we should behave, and these ideas aren't necessarily right or helpful. We have a lot of ineffective, outdated, not useful, and just plain incorrect conditioning (e.g., "If you nag and complain enough, you'll get your way." "Men like women who are submissive." "Everything has to be perfect." "I should be treated like a princess." "You have to watch every penny." "You can never be too beautiful or too rich." "You should tell your partner everything."). And even when a belief is generally true, it's often not true in a specific situation. We don't necessarily notice how ineffective or untrue our conditioning is when the only person we have to answer to is ourselves, but in relationship, the flaws and weaknesses of our conditioning stand out.

The ego hates to be wrong. Even when it plainly is, it hates to admit that to itself and especially to anyone else. This characteristic of the ego is particularly problematic in relationships because it exacerbates and prolongs any conflict over differences. The ego doesn't give up its position easily. Even very rational arguments may be rejected by it because it cares more about being right than about growing or learning.

To allow another point of view to touch us, we have to be interested in growing or at least willing to grow, and the ego isn't, unless that growth serves the ego's immediate purposes. Essence, on the other hand, embraces growth and learning. It's here to do just that, grow and learn, and it welcomes opportunities for doing so.

Have you noticed how growth and learning nearly always involve being humbled? To grow, we have to be humble enough to take on a new viewpoint. Replacing an old viewpoint with a new one is an admission, of sorts, that the old one wasn't the best. This is really hard for the ego to do. When we realize that an old viewpoint doesn't work, we feel the ego's resistance to admitting this. When the ego does give in, we feel its shame and embarrassment, but the growth feels so good and so right that we accept these feelings.

Some people get stuck at this point and choose being right over growth. Their viewpoint remains unshakable and unquestioned. These are not happy people, because life is about growth and evolution on every level—physical, emotional, mental, and spiritual. Life is continually asking us to grow, and when we say no to growth, we suffer because not growing goes against the flow of life, which intends evolution. On the other hand, when we say yes to growth, we become aligned with Essence, and that feels good.

We are rewarded for making this choice by the good feelings that result, despite the humbling of the ego. This humbling is really only a small part of the experience of growth, but if we focus on that, we may not notice how rewarding growth is. We can learn to focus on the good feelings that arise when we say yes to the growth life brings, even if that comes at the expense of some pain and humbling. We can learn to ignore the ego's embarrassment and resistance, and enjoy the rewards of growth in these moments.

So differences are not inherently problematic in relationships. The ego makes differences a problem by taking the position that its conditioning is right and by imposing it on someone else. Conditioning is not a problem until the ego tries to impose its conditioning on others.

Let's suppose you are a woman who likes to have the house very neat and clean, and you are married to a man who doesn't care if the house is kept that way. Is it a problem that you have this conditioning and he has his? No. However, the plot thickens when you decide that he should help you keep the house as clean and neat as you would like. Then you are taking the position that the way you like the house kept is the right way. That position isn't necessarily a problem either. The problem is in imposing this conditioning on your spouse, who feels otherwise. You feel justified in doing this because you feel your way is the right way.

What's likely to happen is that your spouse will argue his point of view about housekeeping in an attempt to resist accommodating your conditioning. Then you are arguing over whose conditioning is right, and there's no possible resolution to that. These conflicts can't be resolved from the level of ego because the ego isn't willing to be wrong and generally isn't willing to compromise. The willingness to see another's point of view and compromise comes from Essence, not the ego, and Essence can't be contacted by remaining in your mind, which is what got you into conflict in the first place.

There is a place in our being where Essence is felt to reside, and that's not in the head but in what many call the spiritual Heart. The spiritual Heart is felt to be located in the middle of the chest, which is why it's referred to as the Heart. When you drop out of your head and into your Heart, you are dropping out of your ideas (conditioning) and into your intuition, which is often sensed in the chest. The intuition is the aspect of our humanness that is connected with the Divine.

The Divine speaks to us through the Heart, and it advocates unity over separation and love over being right. Out of love, it is willing to allow the other to be as he or she is, and it is willing to accept responsibility for its own conditioning. From this place, it's easy to see that you have a choice to either follow your conditioning or not, and to impose this conditioning on others or not. When you are in the Heart, your conditioning isn't that compelling. You see it for what it is—just ideas and not necessarily good ones. Because you can see the truth about your conditioning, it becomes much easier to choose to ignore it, or at least not impose it on your partner.

However, when you are identified with the ego, making these choices is difficult because conditioning feels very real and meaningful and compelling. The conditioning is reinforced by the belief that it is true, which creates more feelings, such as resentment and anger when others don't comply to your conditioning. These feelings make the conditioning feel even more real, important, and compelling. Because you don't want to feel all of these feelings, you try to change the situation by trying to change your partner.

To continue with our example: You are angry your husband doesn't want to help keep the house the way you do, because this feels unfair and because you feel you are right and he is wrong. So you build your case by judging him: "He's a slob. He wasn't brought up right. He doesn't care about me. He's lazy." These conclusions, or stories, seem to lend validity to your conditioning, which is further strengthened by emotions. And these emotions feel very uncomfortable. The ego sees only one solution: The partner must change. Besides, he *should* change because he shouldn't be lazy or a slob, and he should care. You have good reasons for feeling the way you do. You are right; therefore, he must be wrong.

Your partner, however, undoubtedly could come up with equally strong arguments for his case: "There's more to life than cleaning. You're wasting your time. You're compulsive. You shouldn't care what other people think. You should be more accepting and easygoing."

Who's right? You can see why this problem can't be solved from this level. And if you ask someone else what to do, they will just tell you their opinion, which is their conditioning. There are no absolutes when it comes to such things, although the ego thinks there are. The answer to the question, who's right? is that nobody is or everyone is.

Conditioning isn't right or wrong. It just is. It's different from one person to the next, and some is more useful. But there is no one right way to be. That's what makes life so interesting and juicy. How boring it would be if we all thought alike. These differences make the world go around. When you touch into Essence, you realize how much you love these differences, how interesting and sweet they are, and how unique they make each of us. It's only the ego that doesn't like them, and you are not the ego. Wonderful!

Knowing this, you can celebrate (or at least ignore) your differences with others and just let others be the way they are. That is, after all, what you want from them—to be accepted just the way you are.

Essence's Solution to Differences

Essence's solution to differences is to not see them as a problem. Essence doesn't view anything as a problem. When we are aligned with Essence, there are no problems, and that is indeed the reality. The egoic mind spins a false reality, one full of problems that need to be solved. Having problems to solve gives the ego a sense of importance and keeps us identified with the ego because it promises solutions to these problems. Without a problem, we would just rest in Essence because there would be little to think about. Most of our thinking revolves around our conditioning and how to get the world to comply with that—with our desires and dreams—or how to allay our fears, which are also part of our conditioning. Many of our actions are in service to trying to get rid of emotions we don't want to feel, which are also generated by the egoic mind. Our conditioning is behind every so-called problem we think we have.

We don't really *have* problems, but we adopt them. And they serve a purpose for the ego. They give the egoic mind something to do, and when we are identified with it, which we are much of the time when we are think-ing, we feel that we exist as an entity that is separate from Essence. This sense of separation is an illusion, of course, since we cannot be separate from who we really are. Thinking gives the ego a feeling of existing, which isn't actually so. The sense of a separate self comes and goes with thoughts about the *me*. The *me* doesn't exist except as a thought about *me*. The mind is the only thing that can generate this sense of a separate self, so to feel separate from the rest of life, we must be thinking.

This is where Essence comes in. Essence is who you really are. You are what is beyond thought and beyond the mind. The proof of this is that you are aware of your thoughts. Who or what is it that is aware of thought? That is who you are—this Awareness. It can be felt as an energy, an aliveness, a vibration. That's the real you. Take a moment to experience this.

EXERCISE: EXPERIENCING YOUR ALIVENESS

If you drop out of your mind for a moment and into your body, you can experience the aliveness that is a physical reflection of who you really are. The ego resides in the head, but the real you is alive in the body. It is living this body, and it is felt as a vibration, a tingling, a sense of aliveness.

Look at your hands. As you look at your hands, feel how alive they are. It's as if they have a life of their own. They even move on their own. Feel what it's like to have hands. Feel the sensation of having hands and the life in them. This aliveness is present throughout your body. It is the life that is alive in you and living through you. It is who you are. When you put your attention on the sensations of aliveness in your hands or elsewhere, you drop into Essence and the experience of your true Self.

This real you has no problem with anything in existence. It's responsible for creating everything that exists, and it doesn't perceive anything it created as a problem. It purposefully created the diversity and differences that so bother the ego. And it created the ego to be the way it is, so that isn't a problem either. Once you wake up out of the egoic trance, which is also referred to as "the Illusion," you are aware of yourself as Awareness, as Essence. From this place, all is well and unfolding perfectly—perhaps chaotically and unpredictably, but perfectly nonetheless.

Essence doesn't seek to change life, but it does guide it through intention. That's very different from trying to change what has already happened, which is what the ego is all about. Life unfolds according to an overall plan, which adjusts and adapts to our choices. Every moment is different from the last and from the next—that is what's perfect about it. There's no judgment from Essence about each moment, only acceptance. Essence shapes the moment, but it doesn't try to change what already is. It rejoices in shaping it and in the result of that shaping, Essence creates life, which is an ongoing process, but it doesn't argue or lament in what results, as the ego does. It continues to shape life and enjoys this process of creation as it does so.

When we are aligned with Essence, we feel this joy of creation and the fascination and appreciation for what results. Life's diversity and unpredictability make life interesting—and creative, which is where the joy comes from. The creative process—life coming out of life—is enjoyable and fulfilling to Essence, and that's the joy we feel when we drop into Essence. In every moment, Essence is in amazement and wonder at what has been created. Imagine if this were your ongoing attitude as well. It can and will be (and maybe it already is!), once you have moved beyond ego identification, and moving beyond the ego is everyone's destiny.

In the meantime, most people spend varying amounts of time immersed in the ego, which is usually arguing with and complaining about life. To the ego, life is very far from perfect. The ego doesn't appreciate that life was never meant to be perfect. Life was meant to be creative and to evolve its creations, and it's perfectly doing that. But it certainly isn't perfect according to the ego, because the ego has its own standards for perfection, which are unlike Essence's.

Essence doesn't demand perfection, which would be far too static. Essence only demands that things be the way they are—ever changing and evolving into something new. That's Essence's definition of perfection, and that definition is easy to fulfill because that's the only way life can be. Perfection, to the ego, would be the opposite. It would be whatever the ego wanted, regardless of what actually was. This lack of contact with real life as it is actually unfolding is why we are unhappy much of the time. We are unhappy because we are divorced from the joy of Essence as it creates and rejoices in this moment.

Meeting Differences from Essence

Whenever a problem arises between two people, one or both egos are at work creating that problem. Even if only one person is defining something as a problem, it's something the relationship has to deal with. When this happens, it really helps if one person is able to stay aligned with Essence and with the realization that there actually is no problem. This isn't always easy because one person's conditioning tends to trigger the other person's.

Whether both people are identified with the ego or only one is, the way out of the perspective that there is a problem is to realize that conditioning is the cause of the problem and without that conditioning, the problem wouldn't exist. Exploring the conditioning isn't even necessary; just recognizing that conditioning is the source of the problem and being willing to let go of that conditioning is enough. Some conditioning might require some exploration before there is that willingness, but most can just be seen as conditioning and then dropped.

From Essence, differences are acknowledged and not judged. They are seen, and no one takes the stance that his or her conditioning is the correct perspective and someone else's is wrong. Essence, unlike the ego, knows there is no "correct" perspective, only different perspectives. The ego's solution to differences is to try to eliminate them.

We will take a look at how the ego might handle differences in spending money and how Essence might handle them instead. We all have an enormous amount of conditioning around money: what it means, how it should and shouldn't be used, who should make it, whether to save it and how much, whether and what to invest it in and how much, how much to spend on pleasure and fun, how much control each person has over it, and how much discretionary money each person gets. Two people are never going to have identical conditioning around such a complex and highly charged issue as money, so it's no wonder most couples experience conflict around it.

When differences about money (or any other issue) arise in a relationship, generally the first thing that comes up is the question of whose way of dealing with it is the right way. This is the primary pitfall of having differences around any issue. The tendency to argue and build a case for whose conditioning is right is a battle that can't be won and therefore shouldn't be entered into. So the first principle for handling differences is don't try to convince your partner of your point of view. Doing so assumes that your point of view is the right one; however, it's only one point of view and, as such, can't be "the right one."

We are deeply conditioned to believe our point of view and to believe that winning the other person over to it is the correct way to handle these differences. We may even fool ourselves into thinking that it's our duty to get our partner to believe our point of view. We assume he or she will be a better person for it, and we feel it's our duty to make our partner a better person. This is how the ego masks the self-centeredness of its perspective.

This tendency needs to be recognized and curbed before it becomes detrimental to the relationship. Notice when you and your partner are involved in arguing over whose conditioning is right. Here's an example of a problematic dialogue about spending money:

> **He:** I'm thinking of buying a kayak.
>
> **She:** We need to save for retirement, not spend money on more toys.
>
> **He:** You worry too much. We should be enjoying life now, while we can.
>
> **She:** Whenever you buy things like that, they never get used. They just sit in the garage. You've already wasted so much money on stuff like that.
>
> **He:** You're never any fun. You spoil all my fun. You're a drag to be with.
>
> **She:** If you made more money, maybe we'd be able to relax a little and have some fun.

With dialogues like these, two results are possible: One person wins at the other person's expense, or no one wins. Either result is damaging to the relationship because both people have had to come up with judgments and criticisms to support his or her point of view, and that undermines love and trust.

Even if both people manage to avoid belittling, name-calling, and other disparaging types of judgments, some judgments and stories are still bound to be shared in such interchanges. These judgments and stories paint a picture of the partner that leaves out much of the truth. This imaginary image of the partner becomes what we relate to instead of the real partner as he or she is in the moment. In building a case, we create a negative, or just narrow and incomplete, image of him or her, which stays with us and which we relate to. (In the example, he created an image of her as a stick-in-the-mud nag, and she created an image of him as an irresponsible child.) The negative image gets reinforced whenever the partner does something that seems to support it. Over time, it gains strength, and we begin to relate more to the image than to our partner and all of his or her complexity.

This process of creating negative, or just incomplete, images of our partner and relating to those instead of the real person is what causes relationships to deteriorate over time. As in the previous example, if you see your partner as an irresponsible spender, then every time your partner does something that triggers this perception, you become involved with a certain image of him and with a string of judgmental thoughts that go along with that: "He's a spender. He just throws money away. He doesn't know how to handle money." This stimulates feelings of anger, fear, outrage, and more judgments: "He's not such a good person after all. He's weak. He's stupid. He must not care about me. I'm not sure I love him anymore." Now your partner isn't just a spender, but also a bad person who doesn't love you—and maybe you don't love him! Now you have a full-blown story with lots of feelings attached to it. This is what happens when we try to prove that our point of view is right. If you give the ego an inch, it will take a mile, and before you know it, you're no longer feeling any love for your partner.

How are issues like this handled from Essence? Essence allows others to make their own choices about money and about everything else. Being in a relationship with someone doesn't give us license to control him or her. Essence allows the partner to live as he or she chooses to live. It accommodates the partner, although it also may negotiate for what is in its best interest. Here's another way the previous dialogue might have gone:

> **He:** I'm thinking of buying a kayak.
>
> **She:** Do we have the money to do that? (This is a reasonable, straightforward question.)
>
> **He:** I've been thinking about this for some time, and I found a used one that's really a good deal, so yes, we do.
>
> **She:** If that will make you happy, go ahead. (It may or may not make him happy, but that's for him to find out.)

And what does she get out of this? A happy man. And next time she wants something, he's likely to be open to that. Even if she were to suggest they put an equal amount of money away for retirement, he probably would be open to that because he feels good about her for allowing him to do what he wanted—and for being so kind about it. (Some people give in to their partner, but only after they've beaten up the partner with a lot of judgments first.) Kindness breeds kindness. When dialogues go like this, both people end up feeling good about each other, and that can only be good for their relationship.

Judgments and incriminations block love. They don't really stop it because that's impossible. It's our nature to love—unconditionally—but this flow of love gets blocked by judgments, which close our heart to others and make us feel as if we don't love them. If these judgments weren't allowed to grow in this way, love would still be there. Judgments are like a cloud that covers over the light of love so that we no longer experience it. But the love is still there, and it can be uncovered as well.

Uncovering the love that's been hidden by judgments is a matter of seeing the truth about them—that they are just conditioning—and then choosing love instead. To do this can be humbling, so being willing to be humbled is part of this process. To regain love, you have to be willing to see that you were mistaken. The mistake is a completely human one: you thought your conditioning was right, true, meaningful, important, and capable of guiding your life.

Believing this is really not even a mistake because we are programmed to identify with the egoic mind and its conditioning. By doing so, we are perfectly expressing our humanness. However, a time comes for Essence to incarnate more fully in this human form and express itself through it. At a certain point, it's necessary for the ego to step aside and allow Essence to shine through. When this time comes, we are more able and willing to see our conditioning for what it is. Before that, it's very difficult because of our programming.

Working with Dysfunctional Conditioning

Sometimes someone's conditioning is dysfunctional and potentially dangerous, and it may require professional help. Addictive, suicidal, and violent behaviors are some examples of such conditioning. When addiction of any kind is going on, judging, arguing, or trying to convince someone to make other choices isn't going to be effective or helpful. People don't change because we point out what is wrong with them. They don't even change because we want them to. They have to want to change. Every change process is preceded by the desire for change, and this desire can't be imposed or created from the outside.

The ego's way of handling life is generally not helpful because the ego is so self-centered and shortsighted. It doesn't know what is called for in a situation, especially one that involves helping someone. The advice it has to offer will be tainted with self-interest and based on its own conditioning. Essence, on the other hand, knows what is needed in any situation, so the answers to how to help someone lie in Essence.

There's a big difference between trying to change someone to suit our conditioning and thus make us more comfortable in the world and in our relationship, and helping someone change in ways that will actually benefit him or her. The ego tries to do the former, and Essence does the latter. To truly be of service to your partner, your help must come from Essence. And for your partner to receive that help, he or she must be open to it.

There are times when you may just have to accept that your partner isn't ready to change, while being mindful of opportunities when he or she might be open to a new perspective or way of being. Being of help to your partner requires sensitivity to what he or she is willing to receive in the moment. If you try to give your partner insight or advice that you think he or she needs when he or she is not willing to receive it, then what you are offering is likely to appear judgmental, manipulative, or controlling.

Essence is working in everyone's life to bring about the transformation and growth needed. People have free will, and they aren't always willing to accept the ways Essence is attempting to bring this growth about. If they reject one way, Essence will bring another. It often brings this help through other people, who act as mouthpieces for it. When Essence works this way, it does so spontaneously, naturally, purely, and at a time when someone is likely to be open to it.

Essence eventually has its way with us. We all do eventually grow in the ways we need to grow. We can trust that. Sometimes this growth isn't completed in this lifetime, but Essence can wait. We have to have a similar patience with our own and everyone else's process of growth. There's a time for everything, and growth happens in its own time and in its own way.

Sometimes you will be that mouthpiece for Essence, but unless your advice and help come from that place, they aren't likely to be helpful. The greatest assistance you can be to your partner is to be aligned with Essence so that you can present him or her with the love, insight, wisdom, and support he or she needs when he or she is open to it. It's not our responsibility to change or heal our partner, but sometimes Essence enlists our help with this. When we are acting in this capacity, it's apparent because that help feels so right, true, real, spontaneous—and helpful. We *can* help change people from this level, if they are ready to change and willing to take in what we have to offer. Otherwise, it's not useful to try to change them. It's not our business unless Essence makes it our business.

You are not obligated to "go down with the ship" or to stand by and watch your partner self-destruct. When those seem like the only options, you have a powerful tool for change at your disposal—your partner's love for you. When your partner is self-destructing, leaving him or her can be the wake-up call he or she needs. Many a person has been motivated to change by the possibility of a loved one leaving. This can't be an idle threat, however. You have to be prepared to carry it out.

Sometimes leaving is the best thing you can do for someone. It brings that person face-to-face with the consequences of his or her negative actions. It's not useful to you to be a martyr, and martyrdom isn't useful to your partner either. Leaving someone is not a selfish move, but "tough love." By showing someone the consequences of his or her actions, reality brings about lessons and growth.

Making Joint Decisions

Because of differences in conditioning, making joint decisions can be challenging. Two people won't always agree on what to do about things that affect both of them, such as where to live, what house to buy, where to go on vacation, how to invest their savings, how to discipline their children, who will take care of the children, who will do what around the house, and so on. When both people have a stake in the outcome of these decisions, it's important that both have input into them. This is a very different approach from the traditional one, where "the man wears the pants," which often left the woman feeling subservient and unappreciated.

The goal is for both people to feel good about any decision. This may seem impossible, but it is always possible. Although both people may not get their way, a decision can be found that both can live with. Sometimes that decision will be to not make a decision, at least not then. What's important is that the decision is something both can agree on to some extent. If someone is unwilling to go along with a decision, then it shouldn't be made. If an agreeable decision or compromise can't be made, then the couple may be going in the wrong direction. For instance, if you want to move and your partner doesn't, for now moving might not be right for you as a couple.

On the other hand, when two people aren't meant to be together, these kinds of differences can cause a separation that may be the appropriate direction for the relationship. A relationship should serve Essence's goals and each person's direction, and if it isn't doing that, then there may be a reason to question the relationship. This is tricky because we may question our relationship if it's difficult when, in fact, that difficulty is intended by Essence for our growth.

To continue with the example of moving, let's suppose you and your partner agree that you want to move, but you don't agree on where. Here again, if you can't agree on where to move, then it may not be time to move yet. Just because you agree on moving doesn't mean it's the right time to do so. You need to wait until it becomes clear, intuitively, to both of you where to move. You and your partner may not be equally drawn to a place, but you both have to be willing to move there.

Willingness—however great or small—is a good guide in decision making. Are both of you willing to do this? Willingness is an affirmative feeling toward something, and both people need to feel it to avoid resentment later on. This willingness needs to come from Essence, not from the ego's desire to please. The ego sometimes proclaims willingness to please others because it depends on them, but that's not a good reason for agreeing to something.

Willingness that comes from Essence is felt as excitement and a yes about that possibility. This yes doesn't have to be a shout-from-the-rooftops yes; it may be a quiet willingness. But it's free of resentment, resignation, and acquiescence, or agreeing just to keep the peace. This willingness comes from seeing the possibility that this decision is aligned with our own growth and spiritual goals and not just our partner's.

In some cases when a decision is required, compromise is the answer. While two people can't compromise on a decision like moving, because they either move or they don't, they can compromise on decisions like what house to buy. Compromise is a process of examining what is most important to both people about a particular option and trading off some things one person wants for other things the other person wants if there are disagreements. This works fine for many issues, as long as each person gets some of what he or she wants and is happy with that. This last point is crucial because decisions that don't result in both people feeling good aren't good compromises.

Let feeling good be the guide, just as it should be when making more black-and-white decisions: Both people need to feel good about the decision and be willing to abide by that decision. Without that feeling, trouble is likely to show up later on in the form of resentment and blame. Both people have to be willing to take responsibility for the decision so that it won't affect the relationship negatively down the road. If one person feels like he or she is giving up too much or giving in to the other, then that decision shouldn't be made.

Some decisions require education first. Sometimes we argue with our partner over issues that a little education about the issue could solve. An example would be deciding how to discipline a child. Although we would like to think our conditioning and upbringing prepare us for parenting, the truth is that most of us don't naturally have good parenting skills. As a result, arguing over how to raise or discipline a child is often a waste of time—time that would be better spent taking a parenting course or in some other way getting educated about how to parent. It's important to acquire this education together so that both people have a similar understanding, or the arguing may continue.

We also tend to rely on our conditioning to decide on things like who does what around the house. How do couples decide what each other's roles are? Often there isn't enough communication about this. We assume our partner will do certain things and we will do others by virtue of our gender, without clearly defining our roles. The question of who does what around the house is also complicated by the fact that men and women aren't sure these days what each gender's role is or even if there should be such a thing.

Whether the tasks of daily life are divided according to gender or some other criteria, they still need to be divided, and this division needs to be agreed upon. A lack of agreement or clarity can cause little things to become a daily battleground. A key to working it out with your partner is identifying where you have resentments. Resentment over having to do a household task is a red flag that indicates you need to discuss and negotiate the division of labor. You need to work at adjusting these tasks until no one has any resentment. It's very important that the division of labor feels fair to everyone. If it doesn't, resentments will build and get expressed as anger, withdrawal, or denial of affection or other favors.

Here is one approach for dealing with these types of differences:

DIVIDING HOUSEHOLD TASKS AND RESPONSIBILITIES

1. Where do you and your partner agree and disagree about the division of labor? One way to discover this is to ask, "What do I feel resentment about doing?"

2. Make a list of the tasks that bring up resentment in each of you.

3. Examine the conditioning and beliefs about those tasks that are behind the resentment. Maybe you see something as beneath you or not your responsibility as a man or woman. Maybe you see something as part of your role, but that seems unfair to you. Maybe you just don't like doing that task, it's difficult for you, or you aren't very good at it.

4. Would your partner be willing to do that task, or do it at least some of the time? Or would he or she be willing to trade that task for another that you would feel better about doing?

5. If you both don't feel good about doing a task, you could try taking turns doing it, or possibly even hire someone else to do it. It's important that both people feel that the division of labor is fair. Stay with this process until the division feels fair to everyone.

Noticing Resentments

Resentment, like judgment, is an insidious poison to relationships. It seems like a small thing, so we may brush it aside and try to ignore it, or we may hide it because we think we shouldn't be feeling it. What most prevents resentments from being addressed is feeling that it's not okay to ask for help because of some belief or conditioning around roles. For example, a wife may feel she can't ask her husband to help with the laundry because doing the laundry is traditionally a woman's task, yet she may feel resentful over having to bear the burden of that herself day in and day out. In this way, conditioning sometimes prevents us from doing what's healthy for ourselves and our relationship.

If you do nothing about resentment, you miss its value as a message about what you need to retain a feeling of fairness in your relationship. A happy relationship requires a delicate balance of giving and getting. When you feel you are giving more than you are getting—whether you actually are or not—this feeling needs to be discussed with your partner and adjustments made so that the arrangement feels fair to everyone.

If the issue that caused the resentment isn't addressed, the resentment will fester and undermine love and affection. When we feel we are giving too much or not getting enough, we stop giving in various ways, either consciously or unconsciously, and this withdrawal can cause our partner to also withhold from us. Couples often get in standoffs, where neither is willing to give to the other. Not giving becomes a weapon they use against each other. The only way out of this vicious cycle is for someone to begin giving again, but for that to happen, resentment needs to be addressed.

Everyone benefits when resentments are addressed in a relationship, and everyone suffers when they aren't. Your partner will benefit by knowing when you feel resentful because it's not in his or her best interest to have you feel that way. A partner who isn't resentful is a happy one, and a happy partner can only be a boon. Happy partners are loving and readily giving. When one person is loving and readily giving, that inspires the other's love and generosity. Resolving resentments rather than running from them makes it possible for love to flower in relationships.

Negotiating

It may seem odd to be talking about resentment, getting what you want, and negotiating in a book that is as spiritually oriented as this one. Those who are spiritual often think they shouldn't feel resentment or have desires. That's the spiritual ego talking. In spiritually oriented people, the ego often takes on a spiritual guise and becomes a tyrant spiritually. It scolds you for your human reactions: "You must not be that enlightened. Never mind what you want. Forget about your resentment. You should be more enlightened by now." The ego in spiritual guise is just as much of a bully as before. Listening to it only causes you to contract more deeply into ego identification, and that is never good for relationship.

The truth is that if resentment and desire are arising, then that is what's happening in the moment, and they deserve your awareness and attention, not repression. If your conditioning in certain areas hooks you and keeps hooking you, which happens in even very aware and conscious individuals, then it requires some examination. Examination will help you get to the root of your conditioning, and sometimes that conditioning will need to be addressed within the relationship. Some of your conditioning is about you and only you and requires personal reflection, while other conditioning involves others and may require negotiation.

It's true that desire is the cause of suffering. We humans desire, and we suffer as a result of desiring something other than what is appearing right now in this moment. This is absolutely true, and it's also true that some desires need to be expressed within a relationship, because if they aren't, they will cause resentment. If resentment is already present, then the desire behind it needs to be addressed within the relationship if it relates to the relationship, because otherwise it will hurt the relationship. That's a fact of life, of being human, and when our humanity is causing a problem within our relationship, we need to deal with it in a very basic, healthy way: we need to talk about it honestly and fairly with our partner. Most issues that cause resentment are simple issues that can be resolved by discussing what we want and negotiating for it. Here is a summary of how to do that.

DEALING WITH RESENTMENT

1. Notice when you feel resentful. What are you feeling resentful about? What feels unfair? What conditioning is arising around this resentment? You may be telling yourself that you should do something when you don't want to or that you shouldn't ask for help when you would like to have it. You may be trying to do too much or making yourself do something when you need to rest or do something else instead. This may not even be an issue for you and your partner to deal with, but something to deal with within yourself.

2. What desires are behind your resentment? What do you want? Is this something you can do something about, or do you need something from your partner for the situation to feel fair? If what you want is something your partner is capable of giving, what would you like from him or her? What will it take for the situation to seem fair? Define this specifically, for example: "I want the downstairs vacuumed once a week."

3. Bring this issue to the attention of your partner, but not when you are feeling angry and judgmental (when you are identified with the ego). Anger, blame, and judgment will not get you what you want, and they will only hurt the relationship. Wait until you feel loving and warm toward your partner (when you are aligned with Essence).

4. Approach this issue by reminding your partner that you are bringing it up because you care about the relationship, and your resentment is interfering with how you feel about him or her. Enlist your partner's help in solving this relationship issue.

5. Don't tell your partner what you want, but *ask* your partner if he or she is willing to do what you have determined you need to feel better about the relationship: "Are you willing to do that?" If he or she says yes, then finalize the specifics of how your agreement will be carried out, and be very appreciative. If he or she says no, then ask, "What are you willing to do?" Your partner may be willing to do what you want, but not as often as you want, or your partner may be willing to do something else for you in exchange for you continuing to do what you have been doing.

6. Keep negotiating until you arrive at a solution that feels fair to both of you. Don't stop until it does. You should both feel good about the solution and each other. Agree to make some change and then stick to it.

7. Agree to keep the door open for renegotiating if either of you find that what you agreed to doesn't work for you.

8. Be sure to express your appreciation to your partner for being so cooperative. Gratitude goes a long way in a relationship.

A Spiritual Perspective on Common Problems

This chapter presents some common problems in relationships that may cause us to question whether or not we should be in a particular relationship. It's intended to provide a spiritual context for these problems and to shed light on this very difficult question of when to stay in a relationship and when to leave it.

Infidelity

This is a big issue in many relationships. Infidelity is often a sign that something isn't satisfactory within the relationship and whatever is unsatisfactory is not being dealt with. It can also arise because someone by nature finds it difficult to have only one sexual partner. People are unique, and one of the ways they are unique is that some are content with the same sexual partner and some aren't. Some want variety or the freedom to explore forms of relationship other than a monogamous one. Although monogamy is the standard in most cultures today and what is considered moral by most, it isn't natural to some people, and these people often end up unmarried or in serial monogamous relationships.

When someone who isn't naturally monogamous is in a relationship with someone who is, that dissimilarity doesn't bode well for the relationship. The problem is that many who are nonmonogamous assume they are monogamous or hope they are, and they try to fit into the monogamous standard. This situation is difficult for both people and bound to be hurtful. If the one who is monogamous can accept the fact that the other isn't and not take the unfaithfulness personally, then it can be less hurtful. Some couples manage to work out an arrangement within marriage that accommodates the nonmonogamous person. Otherwise, these matches are likely to fail. Everyone is different, and this is certainly one difference that is difficult to overcome.

It's important to realize that although conditioning is just conditioning, some differences in conditioning are extremely difficult to overlook and will be deal breakers in a relationship. Whether they are or not depends on the individuals and their willingness to accommodate differences and overcome their pain, which is always possible, but not necessarily easy.

It's possible to overcome conditioning that makes it difficult to accept someone who is nonmonogamous when you aren't. From Essence, it's possible to accept such a difference and not take it personally. However, for many, this is a very big leap. To think you *should* be spiritually evolved enough to overcome this difference is just another of the ego's judgments. Although relationships are often designed for our growth, certain leaps in growth may be too big to take, at least at a particular time. That would be especially true for those who have some wounding from childhood and find it difficult not to take the unfaithfulness as meaning they are unlovable. Those who are very solidly grounded in Essence and who love themselves and feel complete within themselves might be able to adapt to this situation.

When infidelity is a sign that something is not satisfactory within the relationship, then that dissatisfaction often can be dealt with—and it's a call to deal with whatever is causing dissatisfaction. Instead of dealing with an issue, however, many cope with unhappiness in marriage by having an affair. The affair may make it possible for someone to remain in a marriage, possibly for the sake of children. So infidelity becomes a compromise to divorce. In other cases, infidelity is how someone begins to move out of an unhappy marriage. It's the first step down a slippery slope that often leads to divorce.

There are times when Essence, or the soul, works through the unconscious to create passion between two people that is likely to lead to someone's divorce, if that would benefit the soul's plans of those involved. Falling in love with another person while married happens unexpectedly at times and serves to open up those involved to the possibility of restructuring their lives. The soul can create feelings of falling in love, sometimes even very temporary ones, as a way of moving us out of a marriage that no longer serves our evolution. When this happens, the feelings are compelling and often appear irrational and incomprehensible to others. Infatuation can be like a spell one has fallen under. That feeling of being under a spell is generally a sign of Essence or some other unconscious process. It can cause us to make choices that surprise us and others. Unfortunately, it is impossible to tell if an infatuation is instigated by Essence or simply the result of physical attraction. Such an experience feels quite different from choosing to have an affair because you are unhappy in your marriage, which is generally a more conscious choice.

When people are unhappy in marriage, they often imagine being happy with someone else. They fantasize about someone else, and then when an opportunity arises to fulfill that fantasy, they act upon it. As they imagine a more perfect person for themselves, they begin to withdraw from the person they are with. Their commitment to that relationship weakens as a result of the fantasies and is broken with the affair. Once an affair is entered into, there's often no going back to the relationship if the affair is discovered. Fantasies are destructive to relationships because they cause us to withdraw our energy from the one we are with and put it into someone else. If the fantasizing is extensive, it isn't a very big step from there to an affair.

If you are unhappy in your marriage, then there's an opportunity to examine your conditioning to discover how it's causing that unhappiness. In this way, marriage can be a powerful catalyst for spiritual growth. Rather than focusing on how your partner falls short and looking or longing for someone who doesn't, you examine how your own conditioning is interfering with loving the person you are with just as he or she is. If this person isn't the right one for you to be with, then Essence will move you out of that relationship one way or another. On the other hand, if you are meant to grow in love with that person, then the only way to do that is to overcome your judgments and other conditioned demands that interfere with accepting and loving that person. It's not always easy to determine whether a relationship is meant to be endured and serve our growth or is just not right for you.

What can be confusing is that a relationship may have been right for you at one time, but it is no longer. One of the ways you can tell if it's time to move out of a relationship is if, when you have worked to clear your own conditioning, you still find that relationship stifling and unsupportive emotionally or spiritually. Are you loved by this person? Do you love this person? Or are you just staying together for familiarity, security, or some other practical reason? If you are in a relationship where little love, kindness, and support are shared between you, it may not be possible to turn the relationship around. Sometimes relationships go beyond a point of no return because judgment and criticism have killed love, and love won't be able to return. Respect and trust for each other are key components of love, and if those aren't there, love may not be able to be retrieved.

Inability to Commit

The ego doesn't want to commit to anything—a place, a relationship, a career—because it believes that something better may be possible, and it's willing to forgo what is present for the possibility of something better that isn't present. Essence, on the other hand, is committed to whatever is. It doesn't commit into the future because all that exists is the present, so it commits itself to the present. This is the essential difference between the ego and Essence: the ego dreams of something better in the midst of whatever is, while Essence simply enjoys and commits attention and love to whatever is. In fact, committing attention to anything that is present results in enjoyment. The reason the ego enjoys so little is that it commits attention to what isn't present and to what it doesn't have, and suffers over that, rather than committing attention to whatever is. It loves its fantasies, dreams, and desires more than it loves reality.

To love, we have to fall in love with reality—with what's true right now, not with what might be true in the future or with what we want to be true in the future. Love happens in the now (like everything, really). That's why the ego doesn't know about love—because love is the experience of being in the now, or the present moment, and as soon as the ego experiences the now, it runs. Commitment takes a willingness to fall in love with reality— with the real partner who is in front of you—rather than seek something else, either actually or through fantasy. What you commit to is what's here right now. Who knows what will be here next? All you ever really have is what's here right now, so it makes sense to commit to that—in other words, to give your full attention, your love, to that.

Those who have difficulty committing to a relationship often have difficulty committing to other things as well because they have an underlying belief, or misunderstanding, that what's here isn't good enough and what's somewhere else is better. This is the ego's basic assumption about life: Whatever is happening now isn't *it*. *It* is somewhere else, and *it* is ultimate happiness and contentment. The ego assumes *it* is elsewhere, because the ego perceives whatever is happening as not good enough, and it concludes that must mean there's something else that *will* be good enough. It imagines one day it will find peace and happiness because life will finally line up correctly. Those who can't commit are waiting for life to line up and fall into place, and they're quite sure that what they imagine life will look like then won't look like whatever life looks like now.

The funny thing (or not so funny thing) is that life never does line up for anyone, simply because the ego won't perceive life as ever lining up. The ego has a habit of perceiving life as imperfect, even when it's quite ideal.

In any event, life isn't meant to be perfect or to fulfill the ego's dreams and desires. It serves a higher purpose—one that has very little to do with the ego's fantasies. Life is essentially about learning to love and learning a lot of other things too, and for learning to happen, life is likely to look less than perfect to the ego.

Life brings people to us for various reasons, and sometimes we have to be willing to stretch ourselves to gain what can be gained from a relationship or tap the love that is possible. Relationships, like life, aren't meant to be easy, although they can be deeply rewarding. Commitment makes it possible to tap the potential of a relationship. If you give up on a relationship after the first blush is gone, you may never realize this potential. Sexual union often becomes the glue that keeps people together long enough to begin to experience true love or learn what they need to learn from each other. Nature has a way of bringing about spiritual lessons and spiritual growth. Sexual attraction is one of the ways Essence brings people together and keeps them together long enough to benefit from each other and to grow.

The ego doesn't appreciate growth, and it's not in relationship for that— or for love, really. Its unwillingness to commit and to grow often prevents a relationship that could be a very good one from becoming that. It is forever chasing after the perfect ten, which doesn't exist. But convincing the ego of that is difficult. It believes in its fantasies. To the ego, it's only a matter of time before "the one" shows up. Hope springs eternal.

Essence experiences "the one" in whoever is showing up, and that's the difference between Essence and the ego. It's possible to love whoever shows up in your life. In fact, it's very wise to do that if you want to be happy. If you don't want to be happy, you will reject whoever shows up in your life. This doesn't mean you shouldn't be discriminating. Loving and saying yes to those who show up in your life doesn't mean getting sexually involved with them unless you want to. Essence says yes to them—is open to them—because it is curious. And then it is very wise about getting more involved with them. Essence commits itself to someone only when love is flowing in both directions and the relationship is rewarding on many levels. The ego, on the other hand, may commit out of sexual attraction or because some other need is met through that relationship, neither of which is a good basis for commitment.

Commitment naturally flows from love and appreciation of another. It's the natural outcome of love. And this love is often enough to overcome conditioning and other difficulties that might arise in the relationship. Without love, commitment is hollow and has no basis. Without love, the foundation for the relationship won't be strong enough to weather conditioning and other difficulties.

Commitment only makes sense when there is love, but the ego isn't capable of love. It forms relationships based on needs, and that's when commitment falters. As soon as someone's needs aren't getting met, then the commitment is questioned. Those who are identified with the ego much of the time have a very difficult time committing, while those who are identified with Essence are able to love and therefore able to commit. Eventually everyone learns to love, but relationships can be pretty volatile when egos are in charge. Even so, because relationships provide the ego with many of the practical things it values—sex, security, affection, companionship, support, and help—people who are in relationships for egoic reasons often end up discovering love. This is how life draws people out of the ego and into Essence.

Saving Someone

Many people form a relationship with someone they feel needs saving. The "savior" gets to feel good about himself or herself because the other feels bad about himself or herself. The helper feels superior, special, strong, and good.

Eventually the one who's being saved turns on the savior, and the savior becomes a victim.

These relationships happen largely because of self-esteem issues. They also might be karmic, where one owes something to the other and is repaying it. When the debt is paid, the relationship ends. Savior-victim relationships are doomed to failure because they are not between people who perceive themselves as equals. Nevertheless, they serve the evolution of those involved—until they no longer do.

People often realize they are playing the role of savior or victim, but because taking on that role is a response to unconscious conditioning, they continue until they become conscious of the issue. They inevitably do become conscious of it, and in doing so, they heal the issue. Then the relationship is no longer needed; they've outgrown it.

When people are caught in these savior-victim relationships, they are generally quite unhappy. The strategy of trying to feel good about yourself by saving someone doesn't work and invariably backfires, and the savior eventually is victimized and taken advantage of by the one being helped. Someone who is unconsciously playing the victim doesn't want to be helped and doesn't want to be a victim either, so eventually he or she will resent the helper.

In these types of relationships there's a tremendous amount of guilt, which binds the relationship and keeps it going. The one who is being helped feels guilty for receiving more than he or she is presumably giving, and the one who is presumably giving more than he or she is receiving doesn't feel free to leave because of guilt. Guilt is no reason to stay together, but nevertheless it is why some do stay together.

Those caught in these victim and savior roles are working out psychological issues through their relationship, and relationships at times function as forums for recognizing such issues. They bring unconscious issues into conscious awareness, where the issues can be seen and hopefully healed. Then, once the issues are healed, both individuals are more likely to be able to have a healthier relationship with someone else, either in this lifetime or in another.

The issue that needs healing in the victim-savior relationship is a sense of unworthiness, although other issues may be involved. Unworthiness is perhaps the most common psychological issue. It seems that nearly everyone feels unworthy to some extent. This issue interferes with our being happy in relationships primarily because it keeps us tied to the ego (we are identified with the self-image of being inadequate), and happiness in relationships isn't possible when we are ego identified most of the time. When unworthiness is an issue, one or both people are looking for validation and love from the other, and there's never enough validation and love to satisfy the ego, no matter how generous and loving the other person may be.

When there are psychological issues that need healing, life has a way of bringing us those people who make us aware of our issues and who can hopefully help us heal them. Any relationship is bound to be challenging when someone needs a lot of healing—such as someone who has had an abusive childhood. When we have healing to do, finding the "right" person may not be what is needed as much as making ourselves "right" for relationship is. Sometimes it is necessary for us to be alone to do this healing, and sometimes this healing can be accomplished through relationship. Any relationship, except an abusive one, is bound to bring out the issue and have some healing effect. Life has a way of naturally evolving us.

People often consider leaving a relationship because it's painful. But for some, any relationship would be painful because *they* are in pain, and they bring that pain into the relationship. In these cases, staying in a relationship (as long as it isn't abusive), even though it's not ideal (which it never is), and facing the growth entailed in it may be what's called for rather than leaving, because a relationship with anyone else would probably bring up the same issue.

Commitment has value in keeping people together long enough to overcome some of their conditioning, to heal, and to learn to love someone—anyone. For this reason, there's something to say for commitment even when it's difficult. Just because a relationship is difficult doesn't mean it should be dissolved. If the difficulties aren't faced and dealt with in that relationship, they are likely to have to be dealt with in another.

Having said that, it's also true that many stay in unhealthy relationships that are not conducive to growth. When people are too different, particularly in soul age, there may not be enough understanding and support for them to grow. Relationships that are very negative—ones that have a lot of judgment and possibly abuse—often have a negative spiraling effect on both people, where they seem to take each other down, as does the couple in the play and film *Who's Afraid of Virginia Woolf?* Growth requires a supportive environment, one where our conditioning is accepted to some extent and we are loved in spite of it. If that isn't the case, growth isn't likely to be possible. People can't flourish in an atmosphere of negativity, and they certainly can't heal.

Savers and Spenders

Money causes a lot of problems in relationships. People relate to money differently, and they often want to spend it on different things. How we spend money reflects what we value: if you value beautiful things, you spend money on beautiful things; if you value going places, you spend money on travel. This is one reason similar values are important in relationships. These values determine not only how we spend our money, but also how we spend our time and energy.

Money is a form of energy. Where we put our money is where we are likely to put our energy. Our life and lifestyle reflect our values, and our values determine where we spend our money, time, and energy. If two people are very different in this regard, they are likely to be in a constant struggle over how they spend their money, time, and energy. Each one will resent the other for spending money, time, and energy on something other than on what he or she wants, and each one will probably try to restrict or control the other's spending and activities. A lot of compromising and negotiating—and a lot of love—will be necessary to keep together two people who have very different values.

Our relationship to money is another matter, and it can also be a source of conflict between two people. Some are risk takers or loose with money, while others are safe and frugal with money. Some think a lot about it— they worry, plan, strategize, and study about it—while others think very little about it and are barely aware of its comings and goings. Some are fearful about money, and others are trusting. If two people get together who relate to money very differently, they are going to make each other very uncomfortable. These differences are likely to cause a lot of judgments whenever the subject of money comes up. Of course, these differences, like all differences, are an opportunity for these people to become more aware of their conditioning around money and to recognize it as conditioning. None of this conditioning needs to be a problem. Moving beyond it is challenging, but it is possible, and it may be necessary.

When spenders get together with savers, there may be a reason. There may be some lessons around money or values that they are learning together. Any big difference in a relationship may reflect an issue that is meant to be examined and resolved. If you are being challenged in your relationship to deal with some conditioning around money and values or something else, then that experience must be the right experience.

Whatever you are experiencing in your relationship, you can assume it's the experience you are meant to have, because you're having it! You may be with your partner to model something for him or her, or he or she may be with you to model something for you. One person may be learning from the other, but in all likelihood, you are both learning from each other. You can tell what you are learning or what purpose your relationship is serving for your growth by asking, "How is this relationship or challenge serving my growth?" When each of you has learned what you were meant to learn, you will either stay together and be happy, or move on to other partners.

The subject of money is complicated by the fact that a lot of identity is often tied to it. Savers save money because they want to feel wealthy, and therefore good about themselves, and so that their wealth will be secured. Having money is tied to feeling successful and secure, and they value that *sense* of being successful and secure. Spenders, on the other hand, spend money because they want to have things or experiences that give them pleasure or make them look good. Their identity is tied to having things and experiences and to looking good. They feel good about themselves when they have the right things or experiences or look a certain way to others.

Essentially, both savers and spenders want the same thing—to feel good about themselves—but they go about it in different ways. However, neither way really does the trick. You will never have enough in the bank or enough things or experiences to make the ego feel good because the ego never feels good. To feel good, you have to drop into Essence, and that requires nothing. In fact, things can often get in the way.

If you are able to disengage your identity from money, then money will be less of an issue in your relationship. Having money or not having money doesn't mean anything. It doesn't make you a better or worse person. It doesn't even make you a happier or less happy person. The ego makes money more important than it is. It attaches meaning to money. To the ego, having money means that you are a better, happier, and more success-ful person, and that you'll get what you want in life. But that just isn't so.

When you are living from Essence, your perspective changes, and money loses much of its attraction. It comes and goes, and you realize that much of that coming and going isn't under your control. Money comes to you, and money leaves you. You see that you play a role in that coming and going, of course, but you realize that what you do isn't the whole story. You may pro-vide a service or product, but you have little control over what results from that financially. You do what you can, and the rest is up to life.

The good news is that life is trustworthy, even in financial matters. It brings us exactly the experience we need around money and everything else. If you are experiencing limitation, then that's the right experience for now. If you are experiencing abundance, then that's the right experience for now. Who knows how long that experience will last? No one ever knows. What you can know and trust is that life provides you with the resources, experi-ences, opportunities, and drives to support you and evolve you. So there's no use blaming your partner—or yourself for that matter—for whatever you are experiencing around money.

Our experiences with money, whatever they may be, shape and change our relationship to money and to how we use it. We can be sure of that. The struggles around money are usually about getting and keeping more of it, but how we use it is what is important, and everyone is learning to use it more meaningfully. Eventually we come to see that how the ego uses money is ulti-mately unsatisfying and that Essence will use money very differently. How we use money is not only a reflection of our values, but also of our consciousness.

Different Spiritual or Religious Views

Similar spiritual or religious views are the basis for many relationships. Whether different spiritual or religious views are a problem in a relation-ship depends on a number of things, particularly on how important those views are to the individuals and how tolerant each is of the other's views. Obviously, if two people have very different views, and those views are im-portant to them and held strongly, those two people probably will never get together in the first place. However, what can and often does happen with people who are already together is that one of them might acquire a new view that isn't understood, shared, or accepted by the other.

People can often live quite happily together even when they have very different spiritual or religious views, as long as they are accepting and supportive of the other's freedom to believe what he or she believes. After all, beliefs are just ideas, and they don't need to interfere with love. You can still love and respect others while disagreeing with their beliefs. Whether you are able to do that depends to a large extent on your relationship to your own beliefs. Do you hold them as the true beliefs or more lightly? If you hold them as true and believe it's your duty to convert others, then there will be trouble in paradise. As long as you are identified with your beliefs, meaning you believe they are the *right* ones, you will have trouble in your relationships.

It's essential for those whose spiritual beliefs are of primary importance to them to be in a relationship with someone who shares those beliefs. For those who are intolerant of other beliefs, it is also essential to be in a relationship with someone who believes similarly. To get involved with someone who doesn't share your beliefs when you believe they are the right ones is asking for trouble. It doesn't make sense, but it still happens, often because of physical attraction or because the relationship provides some level of security for one partner or the other.

If people with different spiritual beliefs do get involved with each other, then that's probably the right experience for them! We are meant to learn tolerance, and this situation would bring about either greater tolerance or pain. Pain has a way of teaching things, including tolerance. Struggles over spiritual or religious beliefs in relationships often point to the need for evolution in this area for one or both people. These relationships may not last after one or both people have learned the lesson the relationship was designed to teach.

Relationships that do last are likely to be between people with similar religious or spiritual beliefs. Similar religious beliefs sometimes hold relationships together simply by contract, through marriage vows. Similar spiritual beliefs, on the other hand, may indicate similar values and similar ways of seeing and being in life, and although many other things need to line up as well, these similarities tend to be a good basis for relationship.

Today, people are growing spiritually by leaps and bounds. They are awakening out of the ego, and that awakening can shake up existing relationships. As a result, some people are feeling they are in a relationship they have outgrown, and they are questioning whether that relationship is right for their new phase of life. Of course, there isn't one answer to this question, since every circumstance is different. The answer is eventually revealed by life.

Higher consciousness does require a supportive environment. As much as we'd like to think we are spiritually evolved enough to stay aligned with Essence in any situation or in any relationship, we can't expect to. A negative, unloving, or unsupportive relationship is bound to drag you into ego identification, no matter how aligned with Essence you manage to be when you're not with the other person. If your spiritual values are the most important thing to you (and they might not be), then you'll create a lifestyle that supports living from Essence.

What usually keeps people in negative relationships is fear of the unknown, a need for security, or guilt. These fears and feelings come from the ego, but they can be pretty convincing, even when everything else points to leaving. The questions to ask yourself if you are in this situation are: what is most important to me, and do I trust life enough?

Many find themselves in an in-between place, where they are conscious enough to realize that the old life and relationship don't work for them, but they are not brave enough to trust what they know in their Heart to be true. Eventually, that trust will be developed or the suffering within the current situation will become so great that they will move out of it, if their evolution requires that. Life has a way of moving us forward.

Sexual Differences

Because sexual differences are just differences in conditioning, they don't have to interfere with love, although they often do. Love and sexual attraction are often thought to be the same thing, but they actually have very little to do with each other. You love lots of people you aren't sexually attracted to, and you are sexually attracted to lots of people you don't love. When love and sexual attraction come together, it's wonderful, but a lot of other things have to come together as well to make for a relationship.

Generally speaking, sexuality is more important to relationships at certain times of life than others. When we are younger, sex is often the reason we enter a relationship. As we get older, however, we discover that much more than sex is necessary to keep a relationship going. Other things, such as whether someone is kind, a good listener, a friend, responsible, reliable, interesting, or fun to be with, become very important when we live with someone day to day. Without some of these other things, sexuality isn't enough to create a foundation for a relationship.

What does create a foundation is love, and love comes from respect, trust, and appreciation and enjoyment of each other. These are just as important to sexual compatibility as physical attraction. When people are in love, sex often goes well, whether or not they are physically ideal for each other, because they accept and are at ease with each other. When you love someone, you feel at home with that person, like being with your own Self. People who love each other find ways to enjoy each other sexually even if their sexual conditioning is quite different, and they are willing to accommodate each other's conditioning when necessary. People who love each other want to give to each other and are willing to accept each other's differences and adjust to them. And that makes for good sex.

Sometimes one person tries to retrain the other sexually to accommodate his or her desires. That may work if it can be done in a way that doesn't appear judgmental, which can be pretty tricky. A better way of dealing with different sexual styles might be to go with the flow, to stretch yourself and try out your partner's way of being sexually. For example, if you don't like how your partner kisses, try kissing like he or she does and see what happens. It might be fun, and you might discover that his or her way works for you too. Experiment. Your conditioning is just conditioning. Maybe someone else's is just as good or better. You don't have to change your partner's conditioning to match yours; you can try on your partner's conditioning for size and see if it works for you.

In lieu of that, you can just accept your partner's conditioning and recognize that sexual styles, such as how someone kisses or what turns someone on, are just not that important. You love your partner for being unique. There's no one else like that person. You can learn to fall in love with his or her quirks, imperfect body, or way of doing things because you love that person—the whole unique package. Your partner wouldn't be the same without that bald spot or that crooked tooth. You learn to love your partner not only in spite of those things, but also because of them. When you love someone, anything about him or her can seem adorable, and so it is.

Love sees beyond the costume and beyond the character that your partner is appearing as. Look into your partner's eyes, and see the true Being behind the costume. That's what you fall in love with—not someone's bank account, hair, body, power, or any of the other things the ego values so much. You fall in love with what shines in the eyes, with what is loving you back.

When we love someone from our depths—from Essence—we draw the other's Essence out from hiding so that he or she can more easily express it. This is the greatest gift we can give someone—to create a loving and accepting environment where love can flourish. This kind of connection is what everyone is looking for, and it's available to everyone. You don't need to look a certain way or have anything. But you do have to be willing to drop out of the judging mind and be very present to the person in front of you or, better yet, to the divinity of the person in front of you.

8

EXPERIENCING ONENESS THROUGH ANOTHER

Seeing the Divine in Another

Your partner isn't who you *think* he or she is. Whoever you think your partner is, that is probably who your partner *thinks* he or she is too. But this is just the persona, the personality, the costume for this lifetime. You know the saying, "Don't judge a book by its cover"? There's so much more to people than what we see and even how they behave and what they say. The Being that we are expresses itself in multitudinous ways through all of us, and although these expressions are all precious, they don't really mean anything. We don't even have to like these expressions to love others. In fact, when we like someone, that often just means he or she has a similar expression as ours. Liking isn't a good guide for love, although it has some usefulness in choosing who to be with in relationship.

It's actually possible to love anyone. There are people whose heart doesn't close to anyone, no matter what someone looks like or how someone acts or how different he or she is, because they see beyond the person's disguise to what is Real. The Real—the divine Self—is apparent in everyone if we choose to look for it. It's easier to see it in some people than in others, but it can be seen in the eyes of anyone. The eyes are where it is most easily seen. Everyone knows what it looks like, although not everyone looks for it or chooses to see it.

The divine Self, or Essence, is also experienced as energy, which is felt more easily by some than by others. This energy surrounds and penetrates each of us, invisibly nurturing and sustaining us in this physical form. It contains information about a person's life and experiences and why the person has this form and expression, and when we are very receptive, this energy reveals those things to us. The information isn't received through the mind, but intuitively, through just knowing. This energy contains what we need to open our heart to this person, and that is how it is meant to serve.

This information, which brings understanding, is available to anyone open to it, but the ego isn't open to it because it doesn't want to understand others so that it can love them. Such information isn't really available to those who are identified with the ego most of the time, although they are the ones who need it the most. This is how the illusion is maintained. It's not easy to break free of ego identification and to love. When we do, we feel free and happy. And love, freedom, and happiness are what we all have wanted all along.

Once we drop into Essence and feel love, it seems so easy to love and be at peace. And when we are identified with the ego, it seems so hard to get back to this place of happiness and love. What's the secret, the key, to moving into Essence from the ego? It's always a choice. You *choose* love over whatever the egoic mind is telling you about life, the past, the future, yourself, someone else, or what you should do. You recognize these messages as coming from the ego, and you choose not to listen to them.

Ignoring the ego isn't so easy because listening to the egoic mind is an automatic, deeply entrenched habit. Listening to the mind is the default position for us as human beings. It's what keeps us ensnared in our identity as a human being and in the suffering of the human condition. It keeps us at a level of consciousness where true happiness isn't possible.

It's a good thing we are only playing at being human. We are the divine Self in human disguise, and we have access at any time to divine wisdom and insight, which can show us the way out of our prison of suffering. The trick is we have to choose to notice the wisdom and insight that is being offered by Essence. It talks to us differently than the egoic mind. It speaks quietly and wordlessly through intuition, which often comes through the body and only rarely in words. It isn't enough to receive intuitions—we receive them all the time. We also have to learn to listen to those intuitions in the same way we now listen to the egoic mind. Intuitions can guide us in our lives, and they will lead to much greater happiness than following the ego. Moreover, they will lead us to love.

The egoic mind takes us away from love. It causes separation. When we feel love, Essence is at work, not the ego. Love is how we can recognize Essence. Likewise, separation, contraction, negativity, and the absence of love is how we can recognize the ego. When we feel these, then we know we are identified and being led by the egoic mind, not Essence. It's easy to tell when we are aligned with and listening to the ego and when we are aligned with and listening to Essence. One corresponds to the human condition and suffering, and the other to the divine condition and love.

Relationships are life's opportunity to learn to love. People are brought into our lives to teach us to love. For this reason, many of those close to us (especially family members) are not the easiest people to love. We learn to love by being challenged to love. Life also brings us people who are easy to love, who are a real gift to us because they show us the depth of love we are capable of reaching. Knowing true love with even just one person makes it easier to love others who are not so easy to love.

Oddly enough, our pets give us some of the deepest experiences of love. There is a purity in our relationship with animals that isn't easy to attain in human relationships, which so often remain on the level of the ego. Pets allow us to experience the love that the divine Self has for itself in its various forms and the joy it has in its creations. We allow ourselves to experience Essence in the presence of our pets because we don't need to protect ourselves from them or maintain an identity when we are around them. The ego falls away in the presence of our beloved pets because we identify with them—we see them as part of ourselves, not separate. This sense of unity with life is the experience of Essence, and the experience of Essence is love. Our pets show us what true love is.

Experiencing Essence in Another

We can have this same experience with our human loved ones too. When we are with another, we are most able to experience Essence when thoughts aren't happening or being given our attention and when conditioning isn't being triggered. Thinking can still be happening, but if we aren't paying attention to it, we drop into Essence, and from that place it's possible to experience Essence in someone else, even if that person isn't experiencing it. To experience Essence in another, it's only necessary to experience ourselves as Essence. There is only one Essence, and experiencing ourselves as Essence enables us to experience it in others, however briefly.

If conditioning gets triggered or you become engaged in thinking again, you lose touch with yourself as Essence and with Essence within the other. That's why it's much easier to stay in Essence when the other person is also in Essence, because then that person is less likely to trigger our conditioning or say something that will bring us into identification with the ego. The extent to which both people are able to maintain their alignment with Essence determines the depth of love they will experience.

What often happens is that the ego gets reactivated by the experience of such deep love. It becomes afraid, and then we may say or do something that brings us and our partner out of Essence and back into ego identification. Giving attention to our thoughts and sharing those thoughts is the most common way we lose touch with Essence in the presence of others. This is why silence is practiced at many spiritual retreats. Silence helps us be aware of our thoughts without speaking them or acting on them, and not sharing these thoughts helps others remain detached from their thoughts as well.

The experience of Essence is simple and uncomplicated compared to the experience of thought. Essence is experienced as a quiet, peaceful contentment with life, all of which causes the heart to open and love to flow. This flow of love can be frightening to those who aren't used to experiencing it. Love makes the ego feel vulnerable, weak, and out of control. It only takes a second for the ego to enter into that loving moment, feel this fear, and bring you out of the moment and into your thoughts. Suddenly, you are no longer experiencing the love and the moment, but thinking about them or something else. The love, peace, and contentment of Essence are gone, and you are back in the confusion, fear, and discontentment of the ego.

Staying in Essence with Your Partner

Most people spend little time aligned with Essence when they are around others because allowing ourselves to be vulnerable for long is difficult. Relationships are challenging not only because they trigger our conditioning, but also because, through them, we experience a depth of love that can be frightening.

However, there's a solution to the difficulty of remaining aligned with Essence when we are with others. You can become aware of moving out of Essence as it is happening and choose love instead of the kind of thoughts and conversation that take you out of Essence. You can learn to share only thoughts that are expressions of Essence and not share thoughts that are expressions of the ego. When shared, thoughts that are expressions of the ego interfere with the experience of love and unity. Once you realize this, you can choose to ignore those thoughts and move back into the experience of Essence. Here is an exercise for you and your beloved to try; it will help you explore being in Essence together.

EXERCISE: STAYING IN ESSENCE

Sit across from each other and look into each other's eyes. Don't let any thoughts interfere with experiencing each other in the moment. Continue to focus your attention on the other person's eyes. The divine in the other is right there, looking right back at you. Keep gazing into each other's eyes as if you were gazing into the eyes of the divine, which you are. There is really no difference. Let yourself experience the divine in this way.

Set aside any ideas you have about your partner and what he or she is like, and any other thoughts that define him or her or your relationship. None of these thoughts are real. None has the solidity and realness of the divine presence in front of you. If fear arises, notice that, and go back to drinking in the divine through your beloved's eyes. If thoughts continue to arise, just let them be there, but give your attention to the eyes and the experience of the moment and not to your thoughts.

Continue gazing into one another's eyes for at least twenty minutes. Doing this exercise on a regular basis will make experiencing the divine in your partner easier in everyday moments, and it will strengthen your love for your partner.

Spending time in Essence with your partner will help establish this way of being together. Being identified with the ego is a habit that needs to be counteracted and replaced by a new habit of being identified with Essence together. It takes repeated practice before both people will be comfortable being in each other's presence for longer periods of time without speaking from the level of the ego. From the level of Essence, words come that are often simply expressions of the experience of Essence—expressions of love, appreciation, joy, contentment, peace, and happiness. Beyond this, what is said is only what needs to be said. By spending more time in Essence, we learn to speak from Essence rather than from the ego.

Another benefit of doing this exercise is that distinguishing the ego's words from Essence's words becomes much easier. It becomes obvious that so much of what is spoken isn't only unnecessary, but also divisive, judgmental, and an attempt to know something or to be right. We get some pleasure from expressing these things, but that pleasure is the ego enjoying feeling superior. There's no real joy in that pleasure. Real joy comes from the recognition of our unity with all of life, which is the experience of Essence. Speaking words the ego enjoys keeps us from experiencing the truer and deeper joy that comes from Essence, which doesn't need words. The joy from Essence comes from taking in the experience of the moment, not talking about it.

Overcoming the drive to speak the words the ego wants to speak is the greatest hurdle to staying in Essence and to helping others around you stay in Essence. Speaking the ego's words immediately takes you and those around you out of Essence. So when you make the choice to stay in Essence, you are not only doing so for yourself, but also for others. Silence is indeed golden, but it's very difficult for most of us to maintain. Here are some suggestions for overcoming the tendency to speak from the ego.

Essence in Relationship

Essence is love. To be in Essence is to be in love. If love is what you want (do you?), then being in Essence and staying there is how to have it. The problem is that we have other agendas—other desires—when we are in relationship. Sometimes we want to be right more than we want to experience love. Sometimes we want to be separate and avoid being vulnerable

EXERCISE: OVERCOMING THE TENDENCY TO SPEAK FROM THE EGO

1. Notice your thoughts. Ask of each thought, is it from the ego? If so, don't speak it. The way you know if it's from the ego is if it contains a judgment, opinion, criticism, preference, or belief. These types of thoughts serve to create a separate identity and are intended to make you feel special, superior, or right. The more you do this inquiry, the easier it becomes, but it requires determination and vigilance at first.

2. Do the same with what other people say. If what they are saying to you is from the ego, don't respond from the ego. We often get caught up in identification with the ego because of other people's ego identification. Watch out for this.

3. When you are experiencing Essence, give it a voice: express that gratitude, love, joy, happiness, peace, contentment, and kindness in words. Too often, we hold back these expressions because they make the ego feel vulnerable, when sharing them could bring others into Essence. Words that make others feel good come from Essence.

more than we want to experience love. And sometimes we want what we want more than we want love. It's important to realize that there are reasons why we don't choose love as often as we could. There's a payoff for the ego in not choosing love, and it's good to be aware of what you are trading love for. When we are identified with the ego, other things seem more important than love, because they are more important to the ego than love. That's the catch. *The ego doesn't choose love.*

So what are you to do if you are identified with the ego, but you know Essence enough to want that? That's the situation so many of us find ourselves in. Very few of us live from Essence most of the time. There's an answer, though. When you do choose love, that's Essence choosing love. Essence is able to reach into the egoic state of consciousness and draw you to itself, but you have to be willing to pay attention to Essence instead of the egoic mind. Essence won't shout at you like the mind does. It won't try to convince you, scare you, or bully you to come to it, like the egoic mind does. Essence whispers softly in each moment. It entices you with feelings of love, joy, peace, contentment, and happiness that seep into the egoic state of consciousness. When you pay attention to these feelings, you are paying attention to Essence, and doing that drops you into Essence.

The way out of the egoic state of consciousness and into Essence is not a hard road after all. All it takes is paying attention to the love, joy, peace, contentment, compassion, wisdom, and happiness that are already here in this moment. Can you feel them—any of them—even just a little? That is your doorway into Essence. Even a sliver of love or peace or joy can take you there. Pay attention to that sliver—notice it—and then that will become your experience of the moment instead of your thoughts. Instead of noticing your thoughts, notice these subtle feelings and qualities that belong to Essence, and you are there! Making this choice isn't difficult or unpleasant, but it is a choice.

This is also the answer to finding love in relationship: notice the love that's there and not the other person's persona, words, or actions. This person in front of you is playing a part. Let that part be played, recognize it as a part, and enjoy it. It's all play—*lila,* as the Hindu mystics say: God playing with God in many forms. What fun! Essence enjoys the characters that we are. It accepts them and revels in their quirkiness and uniqueness. It has compassion for their pain and the suffering they bring to themselves and to others. It accepts this pain as part of life too.

Essence accepts whatever your partner is doing or saying because Essence knows that it's not the whole truth of him or her. Essence sees the truth about the other, and it loves the other because the other is itself. To Essence, it's clear that the other is no different from itself. It feels and sees the sameness. It knows only Oneness. It can't be fooled by words, behavior, and looks. Appearances can't totally hide the truth. Look into your beloved's eyes and see.

This is the experience you have to look forward to when you choose Essence over the ego, love over being right or superior, acceptance over judgment, kindness over criticism, and unity over being separate and safe. These are your choices, which can only be made by you. Happiness and love depend on them, but happiness and love can wait. Essence is patient, and it will wait as long as it has to for you to choose it over the ego.

It's time to choose Essence, to choose love. You choose Essence not just for your own happiness or for a happy relationship, but also for peace, love, and happiness for all—for the rest of you in your many guises. You are here to find love, not just for yourself, but also for the divine Self, which has been hiding love from you in this world of form just so that you could have the pleasure and amazement of discovering it in the simple quiet of this moment—and in your beloved's eyes.

About the Author

Gina Lake, M.A. is a spiritual teacher who is devoted to helping others wake up and live in the moment. She has a master's degree in counseling psychology and over twenty years experience supporting people in their spiritual growth. Her books include *Loving in the Moment, Radical Happiness, Living in the Now, Return to Essence, What About Now? Anatomy of Desire, Embracing the Now,* and *Getting Free.* Visit her website at *www.radicalhappiness.com.*

Hampton Roads Publishing Company

. . . for the evolving human spirit

Hampton Roads Publishing Company
publishes books on a variety of subjects,
including spirituality, health, and other
related topics.

For a copy of our latest trade catalog,
call 978-465-0504
or visit our website at *www.hrpub.com*.